ANTICHRIST IS HERE

Russell R. Standish
Health Services
Southeast Asia

Colin D. Standish
President, Hartland Institute
Rapidan, Virginia

Published & Distributed by
Hartland Publications
A Division of Hartland Institute
P. O. Box 1
Rapidan, Virginia 22733

Dedication

In the midst of this world of hypocrisy, there are still a few souls who tread the dusty pathway of life with an eye single to the glory of God. Integrity still keeps these trustworthy individuals faithful to God's direction in their lives. We want to honor such men and women.

This book is affectionately dedicated to Pastor Frank Basham—pastor, evangelist, and, above all, a true friend of both God and man. In spite of the considerable physical problems of Poliomyelitis as a young child, this man followed the calling of the Lord, and trained for the gospel ministry. He gave a lifetime of faithful service, and was gifted with the ever-present vision of the completion of the gospel mission and the return of his blessed Lord. He sought to encourage others with the blessed hope of the Second Coming that he cherished.

Colin is honored to be married to the niece of this minister. He officiated at their wedding in 1963.

This page intentionally left blank.

Acknowledgments

The authors gratefully express their appreciation for the untiring labor of their secretaries, Frances Lundberg and Susan Kuobong, for their painstaking efforts to prepare this manuscript.

This page intentionally left blank.

Antichrist Is Here

Table of Contents

Acknowledgments..3
Dedication..5
Chapter 1..11
    Worldwide Unity Movements
Chapter 2..23
    Who Is the Antichrist?
Chapter 3..35
    Roman Catholicism and the Antichrist
Chapter 4..45
    Early Concepts of the Antichrist
Chapter 5..53
    The Medieval Reign of the Papacy
Chapter 6..69
    Original Sin
Chapter 7..77
    The Papal Record
Chapter 8..85
    The Deadly Wound Is Healed
Chapter 9..95
    All That Dwell Upon the Earth Shall Worship Him
Chapter 10..105
    Globalism and One World Government

Chapter 11...115
European Political Unity

Chapter 12...123
Blasphemous Claims

Chapter 13...133
False Principles of Salvation

Chapter 14...145
The Deadly Wound Re-examined

Chapter 15...159
Seven-Headed Monsters

Chapter 16...167
The Mystery of the Seven Heads

Chapter 17...177
The Ten Horns

Chapter 18...189
The Final Fate of the Antichrist

Chapter 19...197
Future Expectations

Chapter 20...207
The Mark of the Beast and the Seal of God

Chapter 21...219
A Moment to Decide

Chapter 22...231
Come Out of Her, My People

Antichrist Is Here

This page intentionally left blank.

1

Worldwide Unity Movements

In 1956, our in-depth study on the history of Europe in the nineteenth century was a portion of the second year of our history major at the University of Sydney. We were especially interested in the year 1848 because this was the year of revolutions, according to historians. As we reflect upon the history of that era, we recognize that the turmoil and change of that period pales into insignificance when compared with the events of the second half of 1989 and the early months of 1990. Within a period of six months, Poland, Hungary, Czechoslovakia, East Germany, Bulgaria, and Romania had thrown off the shackles of communism. The Soviet Union provided a multiparty political system. The republics of Lithuania, Latvia, and Estonia had also made significant progress toward the attainment of independence from the U.S.S.R. The southern republics of Armenia, Georgia, and Azerbaijan had become unruly.

If we had predicted, on January 1, 1989, that, before that year would close, Poland would install a democratically elected non-communist prime minister; that the hard-line Communist Party in Hungary would be transformed; that East Germany, Czechoslovakia, Bulgaria, Romania, and Hungary would have new presidents; that the Berlin Wall would come down; that East and West Berliners would jointly celebrate the commencement of the new decade; that free passage between the two German republics would be permitted; that Hungary would remove the barbed-wire entanglements and the lookout posts along its common border with Austria; that Czechoslovakia would open its doors for the free exit of its citizens to other countries; that virtually all Eastern European nations would commit themselves to have their own multiparty political systems; that the Lithuanian Communist Party would dissociate itself from the Moscow Communist Party as a first step to independence; that the Estonian Labor Union Organization would separate from its parent organization; that Alexander Dubcek would be restored to a position of leadership in Czechoslovakia; that the U.S.S.R. would officially request papal assistance in the Ukraine; and that Poland and East Germany would officially apologize to the Czechoslovak nation for joining the U.S.S.R. in 1968 during the suppression of the liberalization movement; then we would have been justifiably regarded as wild-eyed speculators. If we had predicted that such changes would be made before the turn of the millennium, we would have been regarded with only a little more credibility; yet all these dramatic events took place in four fateful months.

While the year 1989 saw the unprecedented dismantling of communism in Eastern Europe, the events of that year had an earlier beginning. From the successful Bolshevik Revolution in Russia during 1917, communism was in the vanguard of political change. The defeat of Nazism and Fascism, in the Second World War, and the ruthless negotiation of Joseph Stalin at the Yalta Conference, paved the way for the Soviet Union to assume total control of the destiny of Eastern Europe. Estonia, Lithuania, and Latvia were annexed to the Soviet Union in August 1940, under an agreement with Hitler. Parts of eastern Poland and eastern Romania were absorbed into the Soviet Union. Poland (which included much of what was formerly eastern Germany), Hungary, Czechoslovakia, Romania, Bulgaria, and East Germany became little more than vassal states of the ironfisted Soviet Union. Only Yugoslavia (more liberal) and Albania (more ruthless) adopted a communism that was not directly under Soviet domination. The power and intent of the Soviet Union was demonstrated by its relentless suppression of the liberation efforts which had arisen in Hungary (1956) and Czechoslovakia (1968). When the Berlin Wall was erected in 1961, it became the ultimate symbol of the cold war and the separation of Eastern Europe from the West. The massive arms race was the inevitable result. The Soviets (superpower of the East) and the Americans (superpower of the West) eyed each other with absolute distrust.

Ever since, the Soviets and Americans have tenaciously fought each other all over the world from Korea to Vietnam, Cuba to Nicaragua, Iran to Afghanistan, Angola to Ethiopia, and in other countries. Providentially, none of

these wars developed into a direct conflict between the su-
perpowers. The advance of communism in Asia added to
the alarm in the West. When, by 1951, the communists had
subjugated China, the most populous nation of the world,
one fifth of the people on this planet had joined the
bloodred banner of communism. North Korea, North Vietnam, South Vietnam, Cambodia, Laos, Burma, and Afghanistan   formed   communist   governments.   The
Philippines, Thailand, Indonesia, and Malaysia also fought
wars against communist terrorists. The tentacles of communism were reaching across the planet.

The Americas were not left untouched. Not only Cuba
but much of Central and South America either had communist rule or serious challenges from leftist organizations.
Several African nations, such as Tanzania, Angolia, and
Ethiopia, opted for communist-type governments. It was
not surprising that a high level of neurosis developed in
the Western world, peaking (but not ending) with the Mc-
Carthy years in the United States.

It would be wrong to assume that communism is dead;
yet it is mind-boggling to note the rapid decline of communist powers at the end of the 1980s. Not even the most
optimistic Westerner could have predicted the events of
1989. From Lenin through Konstanin Chernenko, the
Soviet Union had maintained anti-West and antireligion
stances. When Mikhail Gorbachev assumed the leadership
of the U.S.S.R. in 1985, the early efforts of *perestroika* and
glasnost were viewed with extreme skepticism by most
Western politicians and observers; however, as hard-line
Old-Guard leaders lost their leadership roles one after the
other, the new revolution became more believable. This

change of political leadership had not come easily. The gradual increase of freedom came with the resurfacing of old grievances being expressed in demonstrations and riots. The annexed mini-nations of Estonia, Latvia, and Lithuania began demanding greater independence. Armenia, Azerbaijan, and Georgia were each in various stages of social and political upheaval. It was a far cry from the cruel days of Stalin.

The reforms in the Soviet Union encouraged freedom movements in other Eastern European nations. Poland was the first to experience the winds of change. Long before Gorbachev's reforms, the Polish political revolution was taking shape. With the unheard-of establishment of the Solidarity Trade Union, the winds of change were evident. Lech Walesa streaked across the headlines of the newspapers of the world as a meteorite, and assumed the role of a larger-than-life modern hero. Surprisingly, the Soviets of the late 1980s did not follow the policy of military intervention that the Soviets in Hungary and Czechoslavakia had during 1956 and 1968. Without such outside interference, with growing boldness, this movement gained overwhelming popular support.

Following a moderately different course from that of the Polish, the Hungarians began a no-less-determined bloodless coup against their hard-line communist leaders. This time, there were no Soviet tanks or battalions sent to suppress the popular sentiments of the nation. The stage was set for the dramatic events of 1989. These events were fueled by the holding of free elections in Poland where, for the first time in more than four decades, candidates other than red-card-carrying communists were permitted to campaign for elections. As a result, the Solidarity Party swept into power.

Even before this, hard-line communist leaders in Hungary were rapidly losing their influence. A more liberal group of leaders was openly calling for the nation to adopt a Western-style democratic form of socialism. By the middle of 1989, a freedom of expression, unknown for decades, emerged in Hungary. One correspondent testily demanded the return of 40 years of life that he claimed that the communists had taken from him, while others called for a withdrawal of the Soviet troops.

In the last few months of 1989, the existing European scene changed with dramatic rapidity. First, thousands of East Germans demonstrated, forcing their hard-line leader, Erich Honecker, to retire. Thousands of East German citizens found their way to the West via Czechoslovakia and Hungary. In November of 1989, the government began to demolish the Berlin Wall that had been a symbol of hostility and separation since its erection in 1961. Some East Germans even dared to talk of a reunification of Germany, a prospect that not all Western or Eastern nations relished. This soon became such an overwhelmingly popular movement that, by February of 1990, the communist leaders of East Germany accepted it as inevitable. The first free elections of East Germany that were held on March 18, 1990, swept the Conservative Coalition into power, and ensured the reunification of Germany within a very brief period.

Tentative efforts to put down riots and demonstrations proved fruitless; as a result, the authorities were left with the basic option to permit the doors of the nation to open, and grant the right of free exit and entry of its citizens. The mass public demonstrations of East Germany were followed by similar demonstrations in Czechoslovakia. As in East Germany, attempts were made to quell the demonstrations, but the people would not be silenced. Eventually, the nation's long-serving leader, Milos Jakes, was forced to resign. Efforts to reform the system were hastily made, but the populace considered these to be inadequate, as evidenced by the massive demonstrations in their demand for free elections. Alexander Dubcek, the deposed reformer of 1968, became the popular hero of 1989 and the presiding officer of the legislature. The new president was Vaclav Havel, also a longtime hero of reform.

Even more surprising were the changes in hard-core communist Bulgaria. With much less fanfare, the elderly Todor Zhivkov stepped down after 35 years of leadership. There was clear evidence that, behind these rapid changes, Mikhail Gorbachev was encouraging, even insisting, that the reforms of Eastern Europe occur.

But the most tragic events in Romania happened after Nicolae Ceausescu had ruled for 24 years. Ceausescu was a pitiless dictator. In June 1989, when the Chinese had brutally suppressed a student uprising in Tiananmen Square in Beijing, Ceausescu apparently believed that a similar response against a popular uprising against his rule would succeed. This led to thousands of Romanians losing their lives. The revolution could not be stopped, and Ceausescu and his wife were executed on Christmas day, 1989, after a hasty trial.

The dramatic announcement from the Soviet Union (February 7, 1990) that opened the nation to multiparty elections was another evidence of the collapse of European communism.

We can only speculate concerning the influence that these changes will have upon communism in other areas of the world. Despite the fact that the student freedom movement of China was ruthlessly suppressed in June 1989, the question may still be properly posed, "How much longer will this mammoth nation be able to stand against the forces of change?" There can be no disputing the evidence that, in spite of the student suppression, which represented a serious hindrance to these freedom initiatives, China is still in the midst of change. Precedents set in China will undoubtedly affect the policies of other nations such as North Korea and Tanzania, which historically have been greatly influenced by Chinese communism. Tanzania is already showing signs of change after its first leader, President Nyerere, admitted that he may have been wrong in choosing a socialist form of government for his developing nation. North Korea is gradually opening its doors to foreigners. The overtures of Vietnam for aid from the West expresses a worldwide trend.

In the Western hemisphere, national leaders are pondering what these changes in Eastern Europe will mean to Cuba. Even now, communist nations that are not associated with the Warsaw Pact, such as Yugoslavia and Albania, are experiencing growing pressures to establish more liberal policies. One fact is certain: Worldwide communism certainly is declining.

Many Christians have failed to perceive the significant influence that the rise of atheistic communism has had upon the thinking of Protestants as they sought to identify the antichrist power of biblical prophecy. With the rise of communism and its attendant evils, many Bible scholars had their attention drawn away from the Roman Catholic Church which, up to the early twentieth century, had been identified by Protestants as the antichrist. This fact partly accounts for the rapid increase in books that support the futurist interpretation of the antichrist. Futurists teach that antichrist is a single individual reigning at the end of the age. Increasingly, the papacy has adopted the role of the peacemaker and the champion of social justice. When a worldwide survey was conducted in the early 1980s, an overwhelming majority of respondents saw Pope John Paul II as the man who is most likely to bring peace to our planet. U.S. President Ronald Reagan and Soviet General Secretary Yuri V. Andropov, second and third, respectively, were thought to be the next most likely to bring peace to our world.

In February, 1984, in meetings between Reagan and John Paul II, the issue of global peace headed the pope's agenda. This fact is greatly significant. It surely was a remarkable about-face by a power that was known to be the most ruthless suppressor of religious freedom in Europe for more than a thousand years. The ravening wolf now appeared in the garb of a lamb.

This collapse of communism was foreseen and initiated by the papacy.

> In the 1960s . . . one senior Vatican diplomat said,
> "We'll win out against the communists in the next
> generation" (*Our Sunday visitor*, Nov. 26, 1989).

For the last 40 years, it has taken courage and unwavering loyalty to the Word of God for Protestants to identify
the papacy as the antichrist. This power will play the
greatest role in the end-time oppression of God's people.
The euphoria resulting from the changes in Europe will be
short lived. To many, the events in Europe represent con-
siderations of little importance to the average individual in
other parts of the world, but how wrong such an evaluation is! In the Washington *Post* of December 2, 1989, a front
page article reviewed a survey of young Americans. This
survey concluded that these youths viewed the events in
Europe as either confusing or irrelevant to them. It was
clear that parents, teachers, pastors, and politicians are failing to communicate the future impact of these changes in
Europe upon Americans and citizens of other non-
European nations.

The events which have been happening in Eastern
Europe are only part of a worldwide mosaic which is
readying the world for the final climactic fulfillment of
Revelation, chapters 13-18. The Word of God pinpoints
this remarkable movement that is sweeping both the
religious and political worlds as the final effort marshals
the combined forces of the world against Christ and His
faithful remnant people.

On both the religious and political fronts, there are
dramatic moves toward unity. Unfortunately, neither
movement is established upon the biblical principles of

unity which are built upon a truth that sanctifies the soul of man.

> Sanctify them through thy truth: thy word is truth (John 17:17).

> And for their sakes I sanctify myself, that they also might be sanctified through the truth (John 17:19).

> And he gave some, apostles; and some, prophets; and some, evangelists; and some, pastors and teachers; for the perfecting of the saints, for the work of the ministry, for the edifying of the body of Christ: till we all come in the unity of the faith, and of the knowledge of the Son of God, unto a perfect man, unto the measure of the stature of the fulness of Christ: that we henceforth be no more children, tossed to and fro, and carried about with every wind of doctrine, by the sleight of men, and cunning craftiness, whereby they lie in wait to deceive; but speaking the truth in love, may grow up into him in all things, which is the head, even Christ (Ephesians 4:11-15).

> Seeing ye have purified your souls in obeying the truth through the Spirit unto unfeigned love of the brethren, see that ye love one another with a pure heart fervently: being born again, not of corruptible seed, but of incorruptible, by the word of God, which liveth and abideth for ever (1 Peter 1:22, 23).

The unity movements that are fueled by peace initiatives, such as the globalfest that was held in Moscow on January 1990, provide a climate whereby all dissenters are untimately considered enemies of peace and unity. This creates the conditions that are necessary for the great tribulation through which God's faithful people will endure. No doubt, these religious and political leaders who are orchestrating, under the guidance of Satan, these final climactic events of earth's history have no thoughts concerning santifying truth. Both politically and spiritually, the papacy will be acknowledged as the unifying power in the world. At that time, this prophecy will be fulfilled:

> All the world wondered after the beast (Revelation 13:3).

2

Who Is the Antichrist?

Ecclesiastical turmoil was everywhere. The new pope, Urban VI, returned the seat of the papacy to Rome after 70 years of exile in Avignon, France. But many of the cardinals rebelled against Urban's strict discipline. They returned to Avignon and crowned the bishop of Geneva, Robert of Cambray, as Pope Clement VII. Now there were two popes. That year was 1378. For 31 years, both Rome and Avignon continued to elect popes; each claiming to be the vicar of Christ; each claiming to be the infallible successor to Peter; each claiming that the other was the antichrist!

In England, a powerful priest who was the rector of Lutterworth, John Wycliffe, agreed with both of them.

> The fiend no longer reigns in one, but in two priests that men may the more easily overcome them both in Christ's name. Now is antichrist divided, and one part fights against the other (Emma H. Adams. *John Wycliffe*, Pacific Press Publishing Association, Oakland, 1890).

Wycliffe's stand against papal taxation would have led him to the stake if it were not for the powerful friendship of English peers and even the royal court; however, two great Moravian Reformers, John Huss and Jerome of Prague were burned at the stake in Bohemia. They were greatly influenced by Wycliffe.

Identification of the papacy as the antichrist became the constant theme of the Protestant Reformation. Martin Luther believed that the papacy, not an individual pope, was the antichrist. These sentiments were shared by Zwingli, Calvin, Knox, and other Reformers. The following are the comments of just a few of the Reformers. The consensus of their views is striking.

1. *Martin Luther:*

    There sits the man, of whom the apostle wrote (2 Thessalonians 2:3, 4), that will oppose and exalt himself above all that is called God. That man of sin to be revealed, the son of perdition. . . . He suppresses the law of God and exalts his commandments above the commandments of God (LeRoy Froom. *The Prophetic Faith of Our Fathers*, vol. 2, p. 281).

    We here are of the conviction that the papacy is the seat of the true and real antichrist (*ibid.*, p. 256).

2. *John Calvin:*

    I deny him to be the vicar of Christ. . . . He is antichrist—I deny him to be head of the church (*John Calvin Tracts*, vol. l, pp. 219, 220).

3. *John Knox:*

    That tyranny which the pope himself has for so many ages exercised over the church, the very antichrist and son of perdition, of whom Paul speaks (*The Zurich Letters*, p. 199).

4. *Philipp Melanchthon:*

> It is most manifest, and true without any doubt, that the Roman pontiff, with his whole order and kingdom, is very antichrist. . . . Likewise, in 2 Thessalonians 2, Paul clearly says the man of sin will rule in the church by exalting himself above the worship of God (LeRoy Froom. *The Prophetic Faith of Our Fathers,* vol. 2, pp. 296–299).

5. *Sir Isaac Newton:*

> But it [the papacy] was a kingdom of a different kind from the other ten kingdoms (referred to in Daniel 7:7, 8). . . . And such a seer, prophet, and king is the Church of Rome [referring to the little horn of Daniel 7] (Sir Isaac Newton. *Observations on the Prophecies,* p. 75).

6. *John Wesley:*

> Romish papacy, he is, in an emphatical sense, the man of sin (John Wesley, *Antichrist and His Ten Kingdoms,* p. 110).

7. *Samuel Lee* (a seventeenth-century Rhode Island minister):

> It is agreed among all mainlines of the English Church that the Roman pontiff is the antichrist (Samuel Lee. *The Cutting Off of Antichrist,* p. 1.)

The statement from the Westminster Confession of Faith of the Church of England, which was later used by the Presbyterians, is significant:

> There is no other head of the church but the Lord Jesus Christ, nor can the pope of Rome in any sense be head thereof, but is that antichrist, that man of sin and son of perdition that exalteth himself in the church against Christ and all that is called God (*The Westminster Confession of Faith,* Section 6, chapter 25).

The Helvetic Convention of Switzerland mentions the papacy as the predicted antichrist. The Lutheran statement, contained in the Smalcald articles, refers to the pope as the very antichrist who exalts himself and opposes Christ. The 1680 New England Confession of Faith stated that Jesus Christ is the head of the church, and not the pope of Rome, who was identified as the antichrist and the son of perdition.

The identification of the papacy as the antichrist was the focal point of the Reformation.

> These ideas became the dynamic force which drove Luther [and the other Reformers] on in his contest with the papacy (*Encyclopedia Britannica*, 1962 edition, vol. 2, p. 61).

After the initial thrust of the Reformation, the identification of the papacy as the antichrist became less common; however, it was still strong among Protestants of almost all denominations until about the end of the nineteenth century. Today, in the environment of the ecumenical movement, it has certainly become most unpopular to identify the papacy as the antichrist. The majority of Christians prefer to ignore the issue, believing it to be of little importance in today's modern society.

The concept of the antichrist goes far back in history. From the time of the sixth century B.C., when Daniel prophesied about the apostate power that is called the little horn (see Daniel 7:8-11, 24-26; 8:9-12, 23-25), Jews living in the period before the birth of Christ often referred to the coming of the anti-messiah. Some of the Maccabees, a powerful Jewish sect of this period, were convinced that the little horn (the anti-messiah) was fulfilled when the

Seleucid king, Antiochus Epiphanes, desecrated the temple in Jerusalem in the second century B.C., necessitating the rededication of the sanctuary.

Some Christians thought that Emperor Nero (died in A.D. 68), who ruthlessly slaughtered many of the Christians in Rome, might have been the fulfillment of Daniel's prophecy. But the apostle John clarified the matter when he indicated that neither Antiochus Epiphanes nor Nero could fulfill the specifications of the antichrist. Writing about the end of the first century A.D., John identified the antichrist (not as one person) as many people, some of whom were present in his day.

> Little children, it is the last time: and as ye have heard that antichrist shall come, even now are there many antichrists; whereby we know that it is the last time (1 John 2:18).

It surprises many people to learn that the antichrist is mentioned by name only four times in the Bible, and then only by the apostle John (1 John 2:18, 22; 4:3; 2 John 7). But this has not dampened the enthusiasm of Christians who know that the antichrist is the most crucial enemy of truth, salvation, the cross, and of Christ Himself. There has been no shortage of efforts to provide a contemporary identity of the antichrist. During the dreadful years of the Second World War, some even identified Adolf Hitler as the antichrist. Others have identified the great Muslim power and, more recently, atheistic communism as antichrist.

While the term, *antichrist*, is sparingly used in the Scriptures, this apostate power is vividly described in the Bible. Paul uses the terms, the *man of sin* and the *son of perdition*.

He pinpoints the appearance of antichrist as occurring prior to the second coming of Christ.

> Let no man deceive you by any means: for that day shall not come, except there come a falling away first, and that man of sin be revealed, the son of perdition; who opposeth and exalteth himself above all that is called God, or that is worshipped; so that he as God sitteth in the temple of God, shewing himself that he is God (2 Thessalonians 2:3, 4).

In Revelation, John uses different symbolism to identify the antichrist, including the beast, Babylon, and the impure woman.

> And the beast which I saw was like unto a leopard, and his feet were as the feet of a bear, and his mouth as the mouth of a lion: and the dragon gave him his power, and his seat, and great authority (Revelation 13:2).

> And the great city was divided into three parts, and the cities of the nations fell: and great Babylon came in remembrance before God, to give unto her the cup of the wine of the fierceness of his wrath (Revelation 16:19).

> So he carried me away in the spirit into the wilderness: and I saw a woman sit upon a scarlet coloured beast, full of names of blasphemy, having seven heads and ten horns. And the woman was arrayed in purple and scarlet colour, and decked with gold and precious stones and pearls, having a golden cup in her hand full of abominations and filthiness of her fornication: and upon her forehead was a name written, MYSTERY, BABYLON THE GREAT, THE MOTHER OF HARLOTS AND ABOMINATIONS OF THE EARTH (Revelation 17:3–5).

As stated earlier, the Old Testament prophet, Daniel, describes this antichrist power with the symbol of the little horn.

> And he [the little horn] shall speak great words against the most High, and shall wear out the saints of the most High, and think to change times and laws: and they shall be given into his hand until a time and times and the dividing of time (Daniel 7:25).

The century–old question remains. Who or what is antichrist? Is it one individual? Is it a succession of individuals, a nation, or a power? Has the antichrist come? Is he here now, or will he appear in the future?

Many within modern conservative Protestantism look for a satanic individual who appears just prior to the end of the world, who will sit in a rebuilt temple in Jerusalem, blaspheming and desecrating it, and ruthlessly persecuting; however, many Christians cannot accept this position. They discern many statements of Scripture that do not support such an interpretation.

Still others brush the issue of the antichrist aside, declaring it to be unimportant. Such a position is untenable because this power will, Scripture declares, deceive almost all of the world. Such a fact demands that Christians search for an accurate identity of the antichrist power.

It already has been established that the Reformers unitedly identified the papacy as the antichrist. In spite of the planned efforts of the Roman Catholic Church to employ numerous strategies in order to dissuade Protestants from their identification of the antichrist, the identification of the antichrist as the papacy largely remained unshaken.

In his book, *The Church of Rome, the Apostasy* (Presbyterian Board of Publications, 1841), William Cuninghame
specifically identified the papacy as the man of sin and the
antichrist. He pointed to the Roman Catholic Church as
guilty of idolatry, Mary reverence, image worship, and
saint worship (p. 105). He also pointed out numerous instances of blasphemy by the church (pp. 199, 120). He
identified the call to come out of Babylon (Revelation 18:4,
5) as a call out of the Roman Catholic Church (pp. 155-
160).

In 1846, in his book, *Christ and Antichrist*, the former pastor of the Norfolk, Virginia, Presbyterian church, Samuel J.
Cassels, presented one of the most comprehensive reviews
that identified the papacy as the antichrist. This book was
thoroughly endorsed by Presbyterian, Episcopalian,
Methodist, and Baptist leaders of the day; yet, by the end
of the nineteenth century, the identification of the papacy
as the antichrist had been undermined.

In his book, *Christianity and Anti–Christianity in Their
Final Conflict*, Samuel Andrews identified the beast that is
described in Revelation 13 as a cruel and oppressing
secular state. He did not identify it as the papacy, as Protestants, prior to the twentieth century, had consistently identified it. By the earlier part of the twentieth century, the
futurist interpretation of prophecy had almost received
universal acceptance among Protestants; yet there were
still a few Protestants who correctly identified the papacy
as the antichrist. Fred J. Peters, in his work, *The Present Antichrist* (1920), was one of these. He cited the Waldensians,
Huss, Jerome, Luther, Calvin, Sir Isaac Newton, Latimer,
Bunyan, Moody, and Spurgeon as dedicated Christians

who were agreed that the man of sin is the anti-Christian pope. Peters correctly identified the 70-weeks prophecy of Daniel 9 as the 490 years left to the Jews to be God's chosen people.

The Roman Catholic Church determined to dispel the indisputable scriptural evidence of the identity of their church as the antichrist power. They claim, in the futurist view of prophecy, that the antichrist is an individual who will appear only at the end of time, and will cause havoc in the Christian church for a literal period of three and a half years. The futurist view of prophecy, adopted by the Roman Catholic Church, claims that the antichrist is an individual who will appear only at the end of time, and will cause havoc in the Christian church for a literal period of three and a half years.

Today, the futurist view is predominant in mainstream Protestantism. In his book, *His Apocalypse* (1924), John Quincy Adams presented the futurist concept to be the satanic power that will appear at the end of time. This false concept was also supported by F. M. Messenger in his book, *The Coming Superman* (1928). More recently, the futurist view was supported by Herman Hoyt in his book, *The End Time* (Moody Press, 1969).

It has taken time; yet the Jesuits have done an effective work. During the Council of Trent (1545–1563), one of the great burdens of the Roman Catholic bishops was to destroy the influence of the Protestant identification of the Catholic Church as the antichrist. Eventually, the task was given to the newly formed elite intelligentsia, the Jesuits. In 1585, Francisco Ribera contrived his futurist interpretation of prophecy. His whole thesis was that the antichrist was a future personage who, at the end of time, would challenge the power of Christ. And, with great persecution, he would suppress God's people.

The early part of the nineteenth century saw the rise of the Anglo–Catholic movement within the Church of England. The Oxford professor, S. R. Maitland, imbibed and taught the futurist concepts of Ribera in order to muffle the alarmed protest of faithful evangelistic Anglicans against the suggestions of reunification with Rome. (See the next chapter, entitled "Roman Catholicism and the Antichrist.")

The pioneers of the Protestant Reformation were not simply following a concept of retaliation when they identified the Roman Catholic Church as the great antichrist power of prophecy. They were correctly discerning the inspired words of Holy Scripture.

Notice the following reasons why the identification of the antichrist is so important to God's end–time people:

1. So that we will not be deceived by the great effort to unite the world under the banner of this power (Revelation 13:8).

2. That we might seriously take the challenge, of Revelation 18:4, 5, to call God's people out of this apostate religion into the truth of God. True Protestants do not make this identification out of bigotry or hatred; instead, they do it out of love for lost humanity. An integral part of the proclamation of the gospel commission necessitates that men and women be led to the salvation that will free them from the bondage and deception of sin. Today, like no

other time in our history, the identification of the antichrist and the invitation to call men and women out of Babylon must be made.

3. Both the second and third angels' messages, of Revelation, chapter 14, focus upon the fall and destruction of this power and all who serve it. Its identification is necessary to warn the world.

The delinquency of the Christian churches, over the last several decades, to correctly identify the antichrist must be reversed if God's people are to do the work that is necessary in warning men and women before the end of human probation. The invitation of the kingdom of God demands that the warning against the papal antichrist and his work be given.

This page intentionally left blank.

3

Roman Catholicism and the Antichrist

The powerful impact that the Reformers made in identifying the Roman Catholic Church as the antichrist can scarcely be imagined today. As millions of Christians joined the Reform movement, the Roman Church attempted to use methodology that has proven so successful for more than a thousand years in order to eliminate those whom it designated as heretics. With the exception of the isolated communities of faithful Christians (often hidden in the natural fortresses of the earth), the church had been remarkably successful in its persecution. This success had been achieved by the arm of the state, which ruthlessly eliminated millions of those who would not bow to the church's authority.

Historians fail to agree on the number of people who were tortured and martyred for their efforts to uphold pure Bible truth, but estimates range from 50 to 120 million. These men, women, and children lost their lives during the period of papal domination. Almost all of this was done at the hand of secular governments which subserved the designs of the papacy.

The period of the sixteenth century proved different. Sickened by the excesses and corruption of the papacy, many monarchs and rulers embraced the Protestant Reformation, and were no longer vassals of the papacy, obeying its commands; thus, in a number of European countries, the arm of flesh was not available to carry out the Roman Church's dictates. This situation naturally alarmed the Roman Catholic Church. The papacy was not accustomed to this circumstance; therefore, it discerned that a new methodology had to be devised in order to counter the rapid spread of the Reformation which was engulfing Europe. Germany, Switzerland, Holland, Scandinavia, Britain, and other countries generally accepted the messages of the Reformers.

A Spanish soldier, Ignatius Loyola, who had recovered from serious wounds that he sustained in war, established a new order of priests and brothers—*The Society of Jesus,* better known today as the Jesuits. Loyola was born in 1491, just six years after Luther. After meditation in the famous monastery of Montserrat, in the northeastern corner of Spain, he vowed to forsake his former ways and became "a soldier of God." He symbolized this vow by placing his weapons on the altar of the monastery.

With six other young men, he attempted a pilgrimage to Jerusalem in 1537, but was unable to reach his desired destination because of war. As a result, he spent time in Venice, Italy, where he formed his society in 1537. This new

Catholic order was approved by the beleaguered Pope Paul III in 1540. The order was established under the strict organization of a medieval army. Loyola became the first general. Before his death in 1556, the Jesuit order had been established in Spain, Italy, Portugal, France, Germany, parts of South America, and Asia. He was canonized by the Roman Catholic Church in 1622.

Loyola was an intelligent, persuasive leader with a remarkable penchant for clever scheming. His order (the Jesuits) arose during the excitement of the Reformation, and soon attracted some of the most intelligent and ingenious youths of the Roman Catholic Church. This order quickly attained the reputation of containing the intelligentsia of the church. The order's leader was referred to as the *black pope,* and the order became so powerful that there were times when it threatened the very church that its members were pledged to defend. For a time, the order was banned by the church.

The church looked to this new order when it was deprived of the assistance of the civil powers of Europe to enforce its edicts against Protestantism. In an attempt to defend itself against the Protestant Reformation, the Roman Catholic Church called a meeting of one of its most important councils, in 1545, in the small northern Italian city of Trent. The council continued to occasionally meet for 18 years, concluding in 1563. It is generally believed that this council ushered in the beginning of what was known as the Counter–Reformation or the Catholic Reformation. While some reforms were achieved which touched the most blatant abuses of the church, the framework of doctrine and beliefs remained the same.

There were two significant issues of paramount concern—justification by faith (with particular emphasis on its relationship to salvation) and the Protestant identification of the papacy as the antichrist of Scripture. Regarding the topic of justification by faith, the bishops, by majority vote, declared that the gospel incorporated both justification and sanctification. Sadly, they defined sanctification, not as mediated by faith alone, but according to the seven "sacred" sacraments (baptism, confirmation, Mass, extreme unction, penance, marriage, and holy orders); thus the pagan concept of salvation by works was retained.

The subject concerning the antichrist was an altogether different challenge. The arguments of the Protestant Reformers had been so persuasive that even some loyal Roman Catholics were uneasy. It was perceived that debate and dialogue were unlikely to settle the issue; thus it became imperative that the Roman Catholic Church assert a different interpretation of the scriptural prophecy which pinpointed the identity of the antichrist in order to remove attention from the papacy. Realizing that the goal of the recently established Jesuits was to derail the Protestant Reformation by whatever means was possible, their finest young scholars were directed to the task of turning Protestant scholars away from their identification of the papacy as the antichrist.

A satisfying alternative to the Protestant challenge of prophetic interpretation did not come quickly or easily. Eventually, two scholars provided interpretations that were designed to destroy the Protestant identification of the papacy as the antichrist. The first of these interpretations was presented by Francisco Ribera, a Spanish Jesuit.

Ribera applied the prophecies of Revelation, with the exception of the first three chapters, to the future. Antichrist, according to Ribera's commentary that was finished in 1585 and published in 1590, would be a single diabolical individual who would arise at the end of time. He would be received by the Jews, and would reestablish Jerusalem and the temple; further, he would abolish Christianity, revile Christ, and terribly persecute all Christians during his three–and–a–half–year reign. The fact that the futurist view of prophecy was of Jesuit origin will be alarming to many Evangelical Protestants. It deeply concerns many Protestants that the thesis of Ribera is so closely aligned to the modern futurist view that is held by fundamentalist Protestants.

The history concerning the introduction of the futurist interpretation of prophecy into Protestantism underscores the clever and effective work of the Jesuits. Thorough infiltration of the Jesuits' erroneous ideas has robbed Protestantism of its heritage. The work of Ribera took many years to bear fruit in the Protestant community. Its origins in Protestantism can be traced to the forerunners of the Anglo–Catholic movement at Oxford University, in Great Britain, during the early nineteenth century. Ribera's thesis was sent to many of the universities of Europe (including Oxford University) shortly after he had developed it. Led by a small group of Anglicans who were exploring the concept of reunification with Rome, the philosophy of Ribera was rediscovered from this thesis.

More than 200 years after the thesis was sent to the universities, men such as S. R. Maitland, James Todd, and William Burgh were suggesting that the English Church should reunite with the Church of Rome. There was an immediate outcry from Protestant-believing Anglicans who pointed to the Roman Catholic Church as the historic antichrist of prophecy. At this point, the determined scholars of Oxford "dusted off" the thesis of Ribera, and vigorously taught the futurist concept in order to *prove* that the Roman Catholic Church could not justifiably be identified as the antichrist; therefore, it was a safe church with which to unite with. Initially, this turnabout made little impact except in England; thus, as late as the end of the nineteenth century, most Protestant authors in the United States continued to identify the papacy as the antichrist. One hundred years later, the Jesuit interpretation has become so universal that almost all authors, many without any knowledge of the past history of prophetic interpretation, have accepted the futurist concept.

John Darby introduced the futurist view together with the secret rapture (another Jesuit concept) to the United States. He also introduced dispensationalism, and taught a disjunction between law and grace. Darby lived for awhile in Plymouth, England. After studying at Trinity College, in Dublin, he briefly served as an Anglican curate. After joining the Brethren in Dublin, he later established the Plymouth Brethren Church. He accepted, as truth, the doctrine that the antichrist, a satanically controlled world ruler, would appear at the end of the world, and ruthlessly persecute during the period of the great tribulation. Christ would come just prior to the tribulation in order to rapture the faithful Christians (the church). Darby declared that, after three and a half years of persecution by the antichrist, Christ would return to punish the antichrist, and set up His kingdom for a thousand years. Justice, peace, and unity is to reign during that time.

Darby, during six visits to the United States between 1859 and 1874, brought these views to the Americas. Here he found some response from the conservative Protestants who little suspected the Jesuit origin of these interpretations. He also attracted some learned theologians who, though not necessarily accepting his rapture theology, were excited by his teachings. This led to conferences. The first was held in a Presbyterian church, and was followed by conferences in Chicago (1886), Niagara (yearly between 1883 and 1897), and Long Island (1901); however, it took the work of a lawyer who became a preacher, Cyrus Ingerson Scofield, to popularize the futurist view.

When Scofield accepted Christianity, he developed into a persuasive advocate of the futurist interpretation of prophecy. He was a follower of the Plymouth Brethren teachings of John Darby. Soon, he was writing notes and commentaries about the Bible, an idea that he developed at the 1901 Long Island Conference in New York. These explanatory notes were added to certain biblical printings which became famous as did the Scofield Bible. Millions of these Bibles were sold by colporteurs, especially in the southern part of the United States. His interpretations were soon accepted by many with almost the same authority as the Bible itself. It has often been stated that the Scofield Bible has done more than any seminary (some say all seminaries combined) to influence the theology and prophetic interpretation of conservative Protestants in the United States. Today, it is shocking to realize that the

Jesuit concepts are almost without challenge in a large segment of conservative Protestantism.

This review of the Jesuit efforts to defuse the Protestant identification of the papal antichrist would not be complete if we did not refer to the work of Louis de Alcazar. De Alcazar, also a Jesuit, defined what has become known as the preterist view of prophetic interpretation. The preterists believe that Revelation, instead of being a prophetic book, actually sketches events which occured in the era of the Roman Empire; likewise, preterists ascribe the writing of the book of Daniel to a period later than the sixth century B.C., when Daniel lived. They claim that the prophecies of Daniel were written during the time of the early years of the Roman Empire (second century B.C.), and suggest that these describe the persecution of the Jews during the period between the writing of the Old and the New Testaments. As stated earlier, some of the Jewish Maccabees believed that the desecration of the temple, by Antiochus Epiphanes in the second century B.C., represented the abomination of desolation that's cited in the book of Daniel (Daniel 9:27; 11:31; 12:7). De Alcazar and present–day preterists have accepted this interpretation.

The preterist view has had particular appeal to modern scholars and higher critics of the Bible. Such an interpretation eliminates the need for divine revelation and prophetic interpretation. Modernists reject any interpretation that would depend upon divine intervention or divine enlightenment; thus, modernists claim that the prophecies of Daniel were written after, not before, the events.

Neither the futurist nor the preterist views can be sustained in the light of biblical investigation. The concept that the antichrist will be a single individual is an explicit denial of the testimony of John, who identified many antichrists, even in his day.

> Little children, it is the last time: and as ye have heard that antichrist shall come, even now are there many antichrists; whereby we know that it is the last time (1 John 2:18).

Surely, this text alone is sufficient to destroy the futurist concept. Further, the very testimony of Jesus places the abomination of desolation future to His time, thus falsifying the claim that this prophecy of Daniel was fulfilled by Antiochus Epiphanes in the second century B.C.

> When ye therefore shall see the abomination of desolation, spoken of by Daniel the prophet, stand in the holy place, (whoso readeth, let him understand) (Matthew 24:15).

It is extraordinary that, in the light of such texts as these, both the conservative wing (futurism) and the liberal wing (preterism) in Protestantism have so easily been convinced by the deceptive presentations of the Jesuits, whose only objective has been to take the attention away from the Roman Catholic Church. They have certainly not been motivated by a sincere desire to comprehend biblical truth; therefore, we must reject these two schools of prophetic interpretation as unsound and unbiblical.

An unscriptural basis for biblical interpretation of prophecy has been urged upon Protestantism. The climate which has been established, under the pretense of tolerance, makes it most unpopular to identify the an-

tichrist as the Roman Catholic Church. The climate of
ecumenism provides the shield against such identification. To identify Roman Catholicism as the antichrist appears to be unloving and divisive; yet all true followers of
Christ will seek for truth. Though truth will not divide, it
will point out the error that does divide. Those who
proclaim truth are frequently seen as the troublers of Israel.
(See 1 Kings 18:17, 18.)

Sincere Christians will recognize that there is no unity
that is separate from truth; thus, twice in His prayer for
unity, Jesus identifies the truth that sanctifies as a foundation for unity.

> Sanctify them through thy truth: thy word is truth.
> ... And for their sakes I sanctify myself, that they also
> might be sanctified through the truth (John 17:17, 19).

Any other basis for unity is, at best, mere consensus,
and most likely includes compromise; at worst, it is rank
apostasy.

Genuine love demands the identification of the antichrist
power so that no honest person will be deceived, for eter-
nity is at stake. While identifying the Roman Catholic
Church as the antichrist power, we hasten to remind all
sincere Christians that many of Christ's true followers are
still members of that church. They are unaware of the great
deception under which they worship. The Saviour died for
them as well as people of all other faiths. This is the time
for love to be expressed in sincere action as these precious
saints are called out of apostasy into the light of God's
saving truth.

4

Early Concepts of the Antichrist

S amuel Cassels' book, *Christ and Antichrist* (1846), presents some of the most outstanding evidence ever presented to identify the Roman Catholic Church as the antichrist power of prophecy. Cassels, a Presbyterian clergyman who served in Norfolk, Virginia, gained endorsement not only from prominent pastors of his own church but also from Methodists, Baptists, and Episcopalians. His book represents the understanding of the antichrist that was passed down from the great sixteenth-century Reformers, and demonstrates the almost united stand taken by Protestant churches up to and beyond the middle of the nineteenth century. The authors of this book are greatly indebted to the careful research of the Bible, by Samuel Cassels, for many of the insights that are presented here.

Many earlier writers offered insightful definitions of the antichrist.

MacKnight: "One who puts himself in the place of Christ, or who opposes Christ."

Schleusner: "In the books of the New Testament, it [antichrist] always signifies an enemy of Christ and His religion."

No power of the Christian Era has more accurately fulfilled these descriptions than the papal power of Rome.

Cassels, with clear perception, identifies the different names of antichrist in the Bible, reporting this identification as the heritage of the Reformers and Protestants. The names he cited were Paul's man of sin (see 2 Thessalonians 2:2-7), the little horn of Daniel 7 and 8, and the beast of Revelation 13 (Samuel J. Cassels, *Christ and Antichrist*, pp. 12, 13).

It is of the highest significance that some of the early church Fathers in the Roman Catholic Church pinpointed the future antichrist. Of course, these early church Fathers did not understand that these insights were identifying the future direction of the church that they loyally served. We cite representative writings of these thought leaders of the early Christian church as reported by Cassels;

1. *Tertullian* (155–222): He spoke about the future breakup of the Roman Empire, "whose separation into ten kingdoms will bring on antichrist." (The division of the Roman Empire was not completed until A.D. 476.)

2. *Cyril of Jerusalem* (315–386): "There shall arise, at the same time, ten kingdoms of the Romans at different places indeed, the reigning all of them at the same time. After them, the eleventh will be antichrist, who, through magical wickedness, will seize the power of the Romans." The papacy not only took Rome as the seat of its authority, but even took the title of Pontifex Maximus from Pagan Rome for its supreme bishop, the pope.

3. *Jerome* (347–420): "Says the apostle [Paul in the second epistle to the Thessalonians], 'Unless the Roman Empire should first be desolated, and antichrist proceed, Christ will not come.' "

4. *Augustine, bishop of Hippo* (354–430): "It can be doubted by none but that he [Paul] speaks these things [2 Thessalonians 2:2-7] concerning antichrist, and that the day of judgment will not come unless he first appear."

5. *Pope Gregory the Great of Rome* (540–604): "I say confidently therefore, that whosoever calls himself Universal Bishop, or even desires in his pride to be called such, is the forerunner of antichrist."

With perfect accuracy, the early church leaders identified the papacy as the antichrist, little knowing that the church of which they were leaders would actually become the great antichrist power of prophecy, and assume the very characteristics that they had discerned from God's Word.

The concept of the early church Fathers, concerning antichrist, is of great significance. All the church Fathers except Gregory wrote before the complete break–up of the Roman Empire and before the rise of Papal Rome to secular power; thus they did not suspect that they were identifying the very church of which they were a part. It was evident that they expected this power to be another entity. And it is certain that they did not consider the developing papacy to be the antichrist. This fact permitted them much greater objectivity and honesty in detailing the identifying characteristics of the antichrist than later Roman Catholic scholars.

Perhaps the most striking statement of those cited is that of a pope himself, Gregory the Great (Gregory I). Gregory's statement was made in reprimand to John, bishop of Constantinople, who was perceived to be seeking recognition as head of the whole Christian church. John had taken the title of *ecumenical patriarch*. Gregory knew Constantinople well because he had served as papal nuncio to Constantinople from 579 to 584. At this time, there was bitter rivalry between Rome and Constantinople. Rome was the dominant See of the West. And Constantinople had dramatically risen to prominence following the city's founding by Emperor Constantine in the fourth century. Constantinople was, by the time of Gregory the Great, the leading See of the East. This rivalry continued until the eventual separation of the Eastern Orthodox churches from the Roman Catholic Church in 1054. It is ironic to speculate on the fact that Gregory had similar ambitions to those of John, although his response was to call himself the *servant of God's servants*. No doubt, Gregory used his strong admonition as an attempt to weaken the resolve of the bishop of Constantinople.

This statement significantly attests to the fact that, at the time of Gregory's reign as bishop of Rome (590–604), he was not seen as bishop over the whole Christian church. Gregory's statement surely is an effective witness against the claim to the primacy of the bishop of Rome from the time of Peter the apostle; however, it must be acknowledged that, in 533, Emperor Justinian had declared the bishop of Rome to be above the bishop of Constantinople. (See chapter 5, entitled "The Medieval Reign of the Papacy.")

Certainly, the bishop of Rome had already claimed the title of *Pontifex Maximus,* a claim that boasts the right of hierarchical control over all Christendom, if not the entire world. Although the Protestant Reformation seriously weakened the papal authority, the latter part of the twentieth century has witnessed an alarming reversal of the stand of the Reformers so that the pope is now regarded as the head of the Christian church by many Protestants and non-Christians. In evidence of this fact, Anglican Prelate Robert Runcie, archbishop of Canterbury, made a call on October 2, 1989, "for Protestants to accept the pope as universal leader" (Singapore *Straits Times,* Oct. 3, 1989).

Let us analyze Gregory's statement in which he asserts that "he who calls himself Universal Bishop will be the fore-runner of antichrist."

The antichrist is clearly identified as a power of worldwide influence. According to Daniel 7 and 8, it arose out of the Roman Empire. Certainly, the only bishop who claims this today is the bishop of Rome. And his power arose out of the ashes of the Pagan Roman Empire.

It is remarkable how Tertullian, Cyril, Augustine, and Jerome perceptively set forth the timing of the rise of the antichrist. None of them offer a thought for the preterist view that claims a pre–Christian fulfillment of the antichrist prophecy; likewise, there is not the slightest hint in their writings that the antichrist will have a short reign just prior to the return of Christ. It was understood that this antichrist power would exert its powerful influence before the return of Christ. Perhaps Tertullian's statement is the most incisive. He understood that, though the Roman Empire was still of great strength and power during his lifetime, it would divide. And this division would shortly thereafter herald the reign of the antichrist.

The contribution of Cyril of Jerusalem is also very impressive. He saw that the antichrist power would seize and assume the power of Pagan Roman. Had Cyril lived at a later period of history, he surely would he have seen that the papacy was the power which assumed the authority of Pagan Rome.

The statements of Jerome and Augustine are more general than those of Tertullian and Cyril. This, no doubt, is due to the fact that they both lived during the declining years of the Roman Empire. Augustine had misapplied the millennial period to the 1,000 years after the birth of Christ, and believed that Jesus would return in A.D. 1000; thus, when Sylvester II was crowned pope in A.D. 999, it was confidently predicted, by many, that he would be the pope at the time of the Second Coming.

Augustine did not understand the 1260–year reign of the antichrist as recorded in Scripture (Daniel 7:25; 12:7; Revelation 11:2, 3; 12:6, 14; 13:5), and perhaps both Augustine and Jerome were uncertain of the extent of the reign of the antichrist power. (See the chapter that is entitled "Medieval Reign of the Papacy.") Certainly, both were so uncompromisingly Roman in their allegiance that neither would have tolerated the thought that the church which they served was already developing the telltale characteristics of the antichrist of prophecy. Few of the Catholic Fathers did more than these men to sow the seeds of apostasy and paganism in the church with which the antichrist power is now so clearly identified.

Jerome developed the Latin Vulgate Version of the Bible that was built upon the tampered Greek manuscripts of the Western church. In later times, this Bible became the basis of the Douay English Bible of the Roman Catholic Church, and has been the basis upon which the corrupt modern translations of the English Bible (such as the Revised Version, the Revised Standard Version, the New English Bible, and the New International Version) have been derived. Augustine, more than any other church Father, integrated pagan concepts within the Christian church. These pagan teachings contributed to the apostasy of the early Christian church.

The early church Fathers wrote a significant amount of material concerning the antichrist. By the time of the Middle Ages, the term, *antichrist*, was more frequently used as synonymous with antipopes. During the period of the papacy's most blatant excesses, two or more prelates frequently claimed the papal throne. The Roman Catholic Church now identifies 38 such antipopes, but debates still rage in some quarters as to who was the authentic pope and who was the antipope. With the supposed succession of Peter at stake, it has often been a bitter battle. One pope,

Leo VIII (963–965), was initially an antipope, contemporaneously ruling with his predecessor, Pope Benedict V. Later, Leo was elected as an authentic pope. When more than one pope claimed the papal throne, it was common for each to call the other the antipope and, by implication, the antichrist.

The issue of the antichrist was not a doctrine of deep study within the papacy during the Middle Ages; however, after the Protestant challenge, Ribera and De Alcazar presented spurious theories, both carefully designed to deny the scriptural identification of the papacy as the antichrist. Since the Reformation, the Roman Catholic Church has expended much effort to convince Protestants that the Reformers' identification was a result of the contentions of the times in which they lived, and did not reflect the true biblical concept of the antichrist; however, a careful review of the Scriptures re-emphasizes the fact that the Reformers did not simply respond to polemics but to a careful and accurate study of biblical prophecy. These understandings were consistent with those of the apostles and the early church Fathers.

5

The Medieval Reign of the Papacy

The early Christian church greatly suffered at the hands of the pagan world. All of Christ's apostles, except John, suffered the death of martyrdom. At the hand of the diabolical Nero, myriads of innocent Christians were martyred. With varying intensity, later emperors plundered the ranks of the servants of Christ. The words of Jesus were indeed fulfilled.

> Remember the word that I said unto you, The servant is not greater than his lord. If they have persecuted me, they will also persecute you; if they have kept my saying, they will keep yours also. But all these things will they do unto you for my name's sake, because they know not him that sent me (John 15:20, 21).

No doubt, the apostles recalled other words of Jesus which rang in their ears.

> Blessed are ye, when men shall revile you, and per-
> secute you, and shall say all manner of evil against
> you falsely, for my sake. Rejoice, and be exceeding
> glad: for great is your reward in heaven: for so per-
> secuted they the prophets which were before you
> (Matthew 5:11, 12).

Christians were torched, beheaded, thrown to wild
animals, and suffered all sorts of cruel and brutal punish-
ments for their refusal to pay homage to pagan gods.
These refusals were often interpreted as treason against the
emperor. Some models of courage come down to us today.
Perhaps few examples are more moving than that of the
unwavering loyalty of Bishop Polycarp in the second century. As a young man, Polycarp had known the aged
apostle John. At the age of 86, in 155, he was hunted down
like a wild animal and eventually captured. Before the as-
sembled multitudes, he was asked to renounce his loyalty
to Christ by paying respect to the pagan deities. His unwavering faith was passed down to generations through
his words, "Eighty and six years have I served Him
(Christ), and He hath done me no wrong. How then can I
speak evil of my King who saved me?" That day the aged
leader laid down his life, a testimony that he "was faithful
unto death" (Revelation 2:10). No doubt, for him, Christ
has reserved the "crown of righteousness, which the Lord,
the righteous judge" will give him at His second coming (2
Timothy 4:8).

Unquestionably, the persecution reached it fiercest
dimensions during the ten-year period that commenced
during the reign of Emperor Diocletian. This persecution
was foretold in prophecy concerning the church of Smyrna,

as recorded in Revelation 2. The church of Smyrna represented the second period of church history, from the end of the apostolic period (A.D. 100) to the end of the Diocletian persecution (A.D. 313).

> Fear none of those things which thou shalt suffer: behold, the devil shall cast some of you into prison, that ye may be tried; and ye shall have tribulation ten days: be thou faithful unto death, and I will give thee a crown of life (Revelation 2:10).

The ten days of the prophecy symbolize the ten years of this persecution (A.D. 303-313). Though Diocletian abdicated his emperorship in 305, his successor, the ruthless Caesar Galerius, intensified the persecution. On February 23, 303, Diocletian, though married to a Christian, ordered all Christian churches closed, all Scriptures and liturgical books burned, and all Christians placed outside the law of the land. Many Christians were butchered when two mysterious fires destroyed a Roman palace in Nicomedia. Christians were ordered to sacrifice to pagan gods under pain of death if they did not. The tortures were terrible, especially in Egypt, Syria, Tyre, and Palestine.

What Satan was not able to accomplish through persecution, he was able to achieve through the fallible support of Roman rulers. While the Christian church found that it could stand strong when persecuted, it totally failed to meet the test of fidelity when popularity was heaped upon it. In 312, toward the end of the Diocletian persecution, Constantine, then a pagan, marched on Rome. As emperor, Constantine soon saw the political advisability of seeking the loyalty of Christians, and published the Edict of Toleration, which granted religious freedom to Christians. Con-

stantine exempted the clergy from municipal duties and
military service, freed Christian slaves, and legalized be-
quests to the church. The joy of Christians knew no
bounds.

It is not clear when Constantine's allegiance to Christianity began. Even though his mother became an ardent
Christian, he always supported some of the best teachers of
paganism. It is evident that he claimed Christianity well
before his deathbed "baptism."

Constantine's acceptance of Christianity was the first
step toward the union of church and state, a pattern that
was later to characterize the persecution of the papacy
against dissenters. The exercise of state authority was
shortly evidenced. In 321, Constantine mandated the observance of Sunday throughout the Roman Empire. Because
the majority of his officers were still pagans, he enjoined
Sunday worship, not as the Lord's day, but as the day of
the sun; thus he sought to bind his pagan and Christian
subjects together. This step, more than any other, led the
Catholic Church to reject God's Sabbath, and replace it
with the pagan day of worship. Later that century, the
Council of Laodicea (about A.D. 365) admonished Christians to rest on Sunday, in memory of the resurrection;
thus, step by step, the Sabbath (unwaveringly upheld by
the Scriptures and by the apostles of Jesus) was slowly
replaced by the pagan day of worship.

The efforts of the bishop of Rome were not well-received.
Even by the end of the fourth century (except in Rome and
Alexandria), the majority of Christians favored the keeping
of the seventh-day Sabbath. Satan was subtly working to

turn men and women away from the day which alone signifies man's loyalty to the sovereignty of Christ.

The famous Ambrose, bishop of Milan, under whom Augustine trained in the late fourth century, was a Sabbathkeeper; however, he records that, when he traveled to Rome, he worshiped with the Romans on Sunday. Because of this, it was he who originated the saying, "When in Rome, do as the Romans do." It became popular, before the fourth century, to honor Christ on both the seventh and the first days of the week. One was usually treated as the fast day, and the other as the feast day.

In an endeavor to make the biblical Sabbath unpopular, Rome tried to enforce Sabbath as the fast day. But, well into the fifth century, Augustine expressed his displeasure that most of the churches around him kept the Sabbath as the feast day and as their primary day of worship. Of course, it was this ambivalence of worship days that led to the two-day weekend, with a concept that they were both holy days (holidays). Step by determined step, Sunday was enforced on the people as the special day of worship. And, as illiteracy and ignorance developed during the Middle Ages, it became increasingly easier for church leaders to enforce their beliefs and destroy truth.

In spite of the increasingly ruthless attempts to enforce Sunday observance, the majority of Christians, in the first six centuries of the Christian Era, kept Sabbath in accordance with the fourth commandment. In the churches of Asia, including Syria, India, and the Nestorian churches as far away as Siberia and China, the majority of members kept Saturday as the Sabbath. Even Spain kept the Sabbath until the seventh century, as did England. In the areas of Ireland, Scotland, and Wales, Christians steadfastly observed the seventh-day Sabbath until the twelfth century. Even the declaration of Pope Gregory the Great, in A.D. 603, in which he proclaimed that the antichrist would keep Saturday as Sabbath, did not influence vast segments of Christians who were loyal to the Sabbath.

In both England and Scotland, it took the marriage of the rulers to Roman Catholic princesses to bring about the introduction of papal Sunday worship, and ensure its acceptance by the populace. In England, Osway, the most powerful king of England during that time, was the king of Northumbia. He married a Roman Catholic princess. The queen worked with her priestly confessor, Wilfred, who had been well-schooled for four years in Rome, to unsettle the king. To the delight of Wilfred, King Osway called the Council of Whitby on the east coast of York, in 664, to settle the issue. The godly Celtic leader, Caedmon, in Northumbria, answered every falsehood that was presented by Wilfred. But the king, weakened by his marriage, succumbed to the argument that the bishop of Rome was the successor of Peter; therefore, doctrine must be based upon the dictates of the Roman bishop.

The Sabbathkeeping Celtic church of Scotland continued to thrive, albeit often under military attack, until the rule of Malcolm III in the eleventh century. Malcolm himself had been compromised by his education in Roman Catholic England as a young man. There he studied with Prince Edward, who later became the king of England, and was called Confessor. It was his fascination with Margaret, daughter of a former English royal family, that spelled the doom of Sabbathkeepers in Scotland. Margaret was brought up in Roman-Catholic-dominated Hungary, and had purposed to be a nun; however, Malcolm successfully pleaded with her to be his queen. With great zeal, she undertook the task to take over the Celtic church.

Colomba had brought Christianity to Scotland, and established a missionary training school on the western island of Iona five centuries earlier. Failing to discredit the memory of this revered Irish missionary, Queen Margaret turned her attention to the church itself. She was soon effectively discrediting the Celtic church. The queen was supported by her husband, the weak Malcolm III, to call a council which initiated policies that rapidly suppressed Sabbathkeeping in Scotland. The Scottish church was also forced to accept other Roman Catholic religious forms, including the papal form of keeping Easter. She so effectively educated her children that her son, the next king of Scotland, was fully Roman Catholic in his beliefs and edicts.

In every century, God's sovereignty was acknowledged by Sabbathkeepers. Many Waldensians, both in Lombardy (Italy) and Bohemia (Czechoslovakia), were Sabbathkeepers. The Welsh were faithful Sabbathkeepers until the first Roman bishop was seated in 1115. During the twelfth century, Sabbathkeepers were also to be found in England, France, Germany, Hungary, Italy, Bulgaria, and Holland. There were Sabbathkeepers right up to the time of the Reformation in most of these countries. Before the Reformation, reports came from Bohemia (Czechoslovakia), Norway, Russia, Sweden, Liechtenstein, Finland, and Switzerland of Sabbathkeeping citizens.

Many Sabbathkeepers were severely tortured and martyred. Two of the best known Sabbatarian martyrs, of the Reformation period, were Oswald Glait and John James. Glait was a Central European who traveled from place to place preaching the Sabbath truth. He was eventually captured. After a little more than a year in prison, soldiers bound him hand and foot, dragged him through the city, and threw him into the Danube River.

John James, an English Sabbatarian, was arrested Sabbath afternoon, October 19, 1661, while he was preaching. The monarchy had been restored only the previous year, and King Charles II was placed on the throne. James was charged with treason against the king. He was sentenced to be hanged. His body was cut up. His heart was flung into a fire; his head was placed on a post outside the building in which he had preached; and other parts of his body were scattered around the city as a warning to other Sabbathkeeping Christians. The Sabbath, so desecrated by the Roman Catholic Church, comes to us today with a blood-bought heritage.

A number of Sabbatarian Christian churches now exist. These include the Seventh-day Adventist, Seventh Day Baptist, Worldwide Church of God, Church of God and the Seventh Day. Most Protestant churches have unexplainably accepted the counterfeit day of worship—Sunday. Daniel predicted the papacy's attempt to destroy God-established laws and times.

> And he [the apostle little-horn power] shall speak great words against the most High, and shall wear out the saints of the most High, and *think to change times and laws*: and they shall be given into his hand until a

time and times and the dividing of time (Daniel 7:25, emphasis added).

Only the Roman Catholic Church fulfills this prophecy. Its own boastful claims confirm that it has fulfilled this identification as the apostate little horn of Daniel, chapter 7.

> It was the Catholic Church which, by the authority of Jesus Christ, has transferred this rest to the Sunday in remembrance of the resurrection of our Lord. Thus, the observance of Sunday by the Protestants is a homage they pay, in spite of themselves, to the authority of the [Catholic] church (Louis Gaston de Segur, *Plain Talk About the Protestantism of Today*, 1868, p. 225).

> The Catholic Church for over 1,000 years before the existence of a Protestant, by virtue of her divine mission, changed the day from Saturday to Sunday ("The Christian Sabbath," *The Catholic Mirror*, 1893, p. 29).

The Sabbath was only one of the myriad of major doctrinal changes that were introduced by the Catholic Church. None are consistent with Bible truth. In his monumental book, *The Two Babylons*, Alexander Hislop identifies many of the pagan rites which infiltrated the Roman Catholic Church. These include image worship, the Madonna and child, Christmas, Easter, Mass, extreme unction, purgatory, prayer for the dead, relic worship, confession to priests, prayers to saints, christening, the rosary, candles, and the sign of the cross. By the Middle Ages, all these had found a firm place in Roman Catholic worship and liturgy.

Because belief and practices of the church could no longer be substantiated by the Bible, the church claimed authority beyond the Word. It claimed that Christ had instituted such authority in the church, basing this upon Christ's dialogue with Peter.

> And I say also unto thee, That thou art Peter, and upon this rock I will build my church; and the gates of hell shall not prevail against it. And I will give unto thee the keys of the kingdom of heaven: and whatsoever thou shalt bind on earth shall be bound in heaven: and whatsoever thou shalt loose on earth shall be loosed in heaven (Matthew 16:18, 19).

Of course, these words of Jesus, properly understood, were a play on words that indicated the weakness of Peter as compared with Christ. The term, *rock*, referred to in this verse, is not referring to Peter (whose name means a rolling stone) but to Christ Himself. This is made clear by Paul.

> And are built upon the foundation of the apostles and prophets, Jesus Christ himself being the chief corner stone (Ephesians 2:20).

Whenever the church is given primacy over the Word, the church departs from its God-given mission. The Christian church was destroyed by the acceptance of paganism under the guise of church authority.

With the abject ignorance and illiteracy of the majority of the serfs of Europe during the Middle Ages, it was a simple matter for the educated priests to keep the masses of the people in total apostasy; yet, in spite of this, great movements which upheld biblically-based truths resisted the papal oppression. From the early years of Christianity, two great movements, the Celtic and the Waldensian, refused to bow the knee to Babylon worship. Both of these groups of people widely scattered the truth in Europe, and refused to acknowledge the authority of the bishop of Rome. Each sought to teach the people, in their native language, the truths of the Word of God.

Other groups who believed Bible truths later arose, including the Albigenses and the Huguenots. All reforming groups were ruthlessly persecuted. Many adherents were martyred. Without the authority of the Word, the church chose to follow the pattern of Pagan Rome, using its authority to produce conformity by force. As the terrible Inquisitions were instituted, millions lost their lives rather than bow to the pagan apostasy of the church. Once in power, the church exercised the same ruthlessness against dissenters that Pagan Rome had exercised against Christians when it possessed the power.

By the fifth century, the church supported the persecution of those who deviated from the Roman Catholic Church, but it had not yet supported the procedure of putting them to death. Early in the fifth century, Chrysostom advocated every attempt to suppress and silence the so-called "heretics," on the pretext that if this was not undertaken, they would influence others; yet he did not advocate the death penalty. About the same time, Augustine, bishop of Hippo, supported banishment, fines, forfeiting of property, and similar penalties for "heresy," but he did not support the death penalty against dissenters. However, about this same time, pagans began to be murdered by Christian emperors and fanatical Christian mobs. It was not long before Christians were destroying fellow Christians, again by the power and authority of the state. The total numbers that were martyred during the Middle Ages has been estimated between 50 and 120 million individuals.

The Roman Catholic Church has never officially repented of this appalling record.

The medieval reign of the papacy is readily traced to the rule of Emperor Justinian. In 533, Justinian had to decide, once and for all, whether the bishop of Rome or the bishop of Constantinople was the supreme bishop. The bishop of Rome thought he was the authentic pope since his roots could be traced back to the apostle Peter. The bishop of Constanople claimed primacy because of Constantine's transferance of the Roman Empire's seat from Rome to Constantanople in the fourth century. Justinian decided that the bishop of Rome should be acknowledged as the supreme bishop of the church. The reigning bishop of Rome, John II, received the title of Pontifex Maximus (supreme pontiff); however, it was not until 538 that the pope could exercise the power that was bestowed by this title. In that year, the Ostrogoths were expelled from Rome, leaving the way open for the papacy to exert the temporal power that was invested in the pope by his assumption of the title of Pontifex Maximus. By this time, Virgilius was the reigning pope. It is significant that Virgilius, who spent a good deal of his reign in exile, was the first pope who was not canonized by the church. The worldly power that he assumed, on behalf of all subsequent popes, led to a sharp reduction in the number of later popes who have been canonized.

The title, *Pontifex Maximus,* had been bestowed upon Caesar Augustus (the Caesar at the time of the birth of Christ) by the senate in Rome, in appreciation for his strong and peaceful leadership of the Pagan Roman Empire. More than 500 years later, this title was transferred to the pope of Papal Rome; thus began the temporal as well as the ecclesiastical rulership of the papacy. The period during the 1260 years of papal domination of Europe is foretold in Scripture. This 1260 year period is dated from 538, when the pope exercised his newly bestowed authority after the expulsion of the Ostrogoths.

The 1260-day prophecy can be found in Daniel 7:25; 12:7; Revelation 11:2, 3; 12:6, 14; 13:5. Different words and phrases are used for the time period that's covered, such as *time, times, and the dividing of time; one thousand two hundred and three score days;* and *forty and two months.* It must be understood that the Jewish calendar had 30 days in each month and 360 days to the year; thus, each expression, the three and one half years and the forty-two months, consisted of 1260 days. In these prophecies, a day is symbolic of a year. The 1260 years represented the domination of the European world by the papacy (from 538 until the pope was taken prisoner by Napoleon's army in 1798). This was a precise fulfillment of prophecy.

Not only did the Roman Catholic Church ruthlessly persecute in Europe during this period but it also persecuted in all other parts of the world where its influence was felt. When Vasco da Gama, the Portuguese sailor, pioneered the trade routes to India via the south of Africa in 1498, the Catholic Church followed. Its attention was especially attracted to the Thomas Christians on the southwest coast of India, near Goa. Finding Sabbathkeepers there who observed a form of Christianity much closer to that of the apostolic church, the Catholic invaders soon employed the assistance of the new order of the Jesuits to help "convert" these Christians. Overwhelmingly, these believers resisted.

To add further encouragement to the Indians to follow
Catholic practices, the Inquisition was instituted. Unmerci-
ful tortures were experienced. Those who failed to give allegiance to the servants of Rome were burned at the stake.
In an especially brutal way, the executioner first dashed the
blazing torches that were on poles into the faces of these
hapless victims, causing excruciating agony, until their
faces were burned to cinders. Next, they lighted the fagots
at the feet of these faithful Christians (B. G. Wilkinson.
Truth Triumphant, Leaves of Autumn, Payson, AZ, 1985, p.
319).

In like manner, the Portuguese pitilessly persecuted the
Muslims of Java. The people were often left with only two
alternatives—accept Catholicism or die. Naturally, the
majority chose Catholicism; thus, at gunpoint and sword,
many instant "Christian conversions" were made. In the
New World, the church was no less ruthless. In places
such as Guatemala and Peru, the persecutions of the
Spanish Inquisition were felt with ruthless ferocity.

To a major extent, after the fall of the papacy in 1798,
there was less papal persecution because the church no
longer had the power of the state to enforce its heartless
edicts. The Word of God clearly states that the restored
papacy will again become a powerful persecuting agent.

> And that no man might buy or sell, save he that had
> the mark, or the name of the beast, or the number of
> his name (Revelation 13:17).
>
> And he had power to give life unto the image of the
> beast, that the image of the beast should both speak,
> and cause that as many as would not worship the
> image of the beast should be killed (Revelation 13:15).

Once again, Catholicism, assisted by apostate Protestantism, will enforce its edicts by the arm of the civil law. (See chapter 9, entitled "And All That Dwell Upon the Earth Shall Worship Him.") It will require a return to true loyalty to God's Word and a true submission to Christ if His people are to remain faithful under such persecution. Now is the time to find the power of the indwelling Christ in order to gain victory over every wrong word and action, so that, when the ultimate test comes, we will unflinchingly remain loyal to Christ.

This page intentionally left blank.

6

Original Sin

The doctrine of original sin has influenced the teachings of Roman Catholicism more than any other concept. In introducing this false doctrine into the Christian church, Augustine, the bishop of Hippo, declared that a baby, from the moment of conception, is guilty of the original sin of Adam. This guilt at conception merits eternal torment in hell for that child. Augustine, borrowing from pagan doctrine, asserted that "baptism" alone purified an infant from original sin; thus God was represented as an unjust monster who torments those that He has given life to if their parents carelessly omit to have them sprinkled. This damnable doctrine specifically challenges the plain words of Scripture.

> The soul that sinneth, it shall die. The son shall not bear the iniquity of the father, neither shall the father bear the iniquity of the son: the righteousness of the righteous shall be upon him, and the wickedness of the wicked shall be upon him (Ezekiel 18:20).

No one is punished for the sins of his father; yet, despite the contrary testimony of Scripture, some popes made even more absurd pronouncements.

> Innocent I (401-417) wrote to the Council of Milevis and Galasius I (492-496) wrote to the bishops of Picenum that babies were obliged to receive communion. If they died baptized but uncommunicated, they would go straight to hell (Peter de Rosa, *Vicars of Christ*, p. 289).

The concept that babies who had died before recieving communion were in hell was finally rejected by the Council of Trent in the sixteenth century; however, this concept of eternal torment for babies is still held.

The doctrine of original sin has popularized the false form of baptism that sprinkles infants with water. This eventually led the vast majority of Christians to forsake the biblical doctrine of adult (believer) baptism which is performed by full immersion. Pope Gregory believed Augustine's error.

> Gregory the Great said that unbaptized babies go straight to hell, and suffer there for eternity (*ibid.*).

Catholics faced heavy strains upon the marriage relationship, as ordained of God, when they accepted the view (prevalent in some pagan societies) that sexual relations in marriage was sinful. Prelates were always ready to defend it even when attempts were made to demonstrate the inconsistency of the doctrine of original sin.

> Gregory [the Great] was not blind to the problem this [the doctrine of original sin] raised. For example, parents were cleansed from original sin in baptism. How could they hand down original sin to their babies? He answers: Though holy themselves, they

handed down corrupt nature through sex, desire gal-
vanized by lust. Babies are born as the damned fruit
of the lust of their redeemed parents. From the first,
they are the offspring of Gehenna, or Hell; they are
just children of wrath because they are sinners. If they
die unbaptized, they are condemned to everlasting
torment for the guilt of their birth alone. Existence is
itself a state of sin; to be born is to qualify for eternal
punishment (*ibid.*, p. 452).

Another inconsistency concerned the incarnation of
Christ. He certainly did not possess a nature that was con-
taminated by original sin. Since He was conceived of the
Holy Spirit, it was asserted that He was free of original sin
because no sex was involved. But, in order to distance
Jesus further from original sin, the doctrine of the Immaculate Conception of Mary was fabricated. Mary was also
stated to be born of a virgin and conceived of the Holy
Spirit.

Until the twelfth century, Christians took it for
granted that Mary was conceived in original sin. Pope
Gregory the Great emphatically said that "Christ
alone was conceived without sin." Again and again,
he said all human beings are sinful, even the holiest,
with the sole exception of Christ. His reasoning and
that of all the Fathers leaves no doubt in the matter.
The sex act *always* involved sin. Mary was conceived
normally, *therefore* in sin; Jesus was conceived vir-
ginally, *therefore* without original sin . . . The cult of
the virgin developed apace in the Middle Ages.
Catholics tended to lose sight of the humanness of
Christ [because of the false view that His human nature differed from ours]; as a result, He appeared
remote, not so much the Mediator between God and
men as God Himself. This created the need for a

mediator with the Mediator, someone holy and powerful. The rise of Mariology coincided with the decline of Christology *(ibid.,* pp., 332, 333).

Unfortunately, the doctrine that Christ's human nature differed from ours led to loss of faith in His mediatorial work on behalf of mankind.

> For there is one God, and one mediator between God and men, the man Christ Jesus (1 Timothy 2:5).

The reason that Christ's mediatorial role has been usurped by priests and saints is because the doctrine of original sin has removed Christ as our High Priest and replaced Him with human priests. Jesus' qualification as our High Priest depends upon His possession of our nature.

> For verily he took not on him the nature of angels; but he took on him the seed of Abraham. Wherefore in all things it behoved him to be made like unto his brethren, that he might be a merciful and faithful high priest in things pertaining to God, to make reconciliation for the sins of the people. For in that he himself hath suffered being tempted, he is able to succour them that are tempted (Hebrews 2:16-18).

Christ was made like His brethren in *all* things. By postulating the notion that Christ was made different from mankind, the Roman Catholic Church deprived Christ of His right to be our High Priest. No man is born with original sin, but all are born with sin-weakened natures. Christ was also born with a sin-weakened nature, as Scripture testifies.

> Concerning his Son Jesus Christ our Lord, which was made of the seed of David according to the flesh (Romans 1:3).

> For what the law could not do, in that it was weak through the flesh, God sending his own Son in the likeness of sinful flesh, and for sin, condemned sin in the flesh (Romans 8:3).

Christ could not have been tempted as we are if He possessed a human nature that was different from ours. He assures us that He indeed understands our human feelings and infirmities because, as a man, He was tempted as we are; yet He did not sin.

> For we have not an high priest which cannot be touched with the feeling of our infirmities; but was in all points tempted like as we are, yet without sin (Hebrews 4:15).

The doctrine of original sin also led to the declaration that those who had never heard the gospel would all perish in eternal hell.

> It is not as if pontiffs and Fathers said that they did not know how babies were saved; they categorically said it was impossible. They did not plead ignorance of the fate of the mass of mankind who had never heard of Christ; instead, they affirmed, without qualification, that they all went to hell. There was no salvation outside the church (by the church, they meant the Catholic Church wherein entry was gained *only* by baptism of water). These views were repeated century after century without one dissenting voice. It was Catholic teaching, taught always, everywhere by everyone. We noticed that when Francis Xavier went to the Indies he was certain that unbaptized pagans, *however virtuous*, could not get to heaven (Peter de Rosa, *Vicars of Christ*, p. 460).

Notice what the Scriptures quote Jesus as saying concerning this issue:

If ye were blind, ye should have no sin (John 9:41).

When Paul spoke on Mars Hill, in Athens, Greece, he referred to the former ignorance of the Greeks in matters that partained to the gospel.

And the times of this ignorance God winked at (Acts 17:30).

Paul also revealed God's attitude toward all people and their relationship to His law in his epistle to the believers in Rome.

For there is no respect of persons with God. For as many as have sinned without law shall also perish without law: and as many as have sinned in the law shall be judged by the law; (For not the hearers of the law are just before God, but the doers of the law shall be justified. For when the Gentiles, which have not the law, do by nature the things contained in the law, these, having not the law, are a law unto themselves: which shew the work of the law written in their hearts, their conscience also bearing witness, and their thoughts the mean while accusing or else excusing one another;) in the day when God shall judge the secrets of men by Jesus Christ according to my gospel (Romans 2:11-16).

Those who are ignorant of the gospel message are judged according to their response to the minimal light that they possess. Some will obtain eternal life. Jesus died for the salvation of the whole world. He does not want anyone to perish even though some souls will choose to disobey the light that they have received and will perish.

The Lord . . . is longsuffering to us-ward, not willing that any should perish, but that all should come to repentance (2 Peter 3:9).

The doctrine of original sin, a doctrine that is not found anywhere in Scripture, has been the mother of the most vile doctrines ever to enter the Christian church. These vile and unscriptual doctrines are eternal torment of unbaptized babies, the concept of limbo (created in order to soften this first doctrine of eternal torment of unbaptized babies), the sinfulness of the sexual relationship in marriage, the immaculate conception of Mary, the denial of the true human nature of Jesus, the acceptance of confession to priests, the denial of Christ's mediatorial and High Priestly ministry, the ritual of infant baptism, and the notion that those who have never heard the Christian message are, by that fact alone, excluded from eternal life.

Perhaps W.E.H. Lecky, in his book *History of European Morals*, as quoted by Peter de Rosa, in his comments upon the "fate" of unbaptized babies (that are assumed to have died while still in possession of original sin) elegantly sums up the foundation of the doctrine of original sin.

> That a little child who lives but a few minutes after birth and dies before it has been sprinkled with the sacred water is, in such a sense, responsible for its ancestor having six thousand years before eaten a forbidden fruit; that it may, with perfect justice, be resuscitated and cast into the abyss of eternal fire in expiation of this ancestral crime; that an all-righteous and merciful Creator, in the full exercise of these attributes, deliberately calls into existence sentient [sensitive] beings whom he had, from eternity, irrevocably destined to endure unspeakable, unmitigated torture are propositions which are at once so extravagantly absurd and so ineffably [indescribably] atrocious that their adoption might well lead men to doubt the universality of moral perception. Such teaching is, in

fact, simply demonism, and demonism in its most extreme form (quoted in Peter de Rosa, *Vicars of Christ*, p. 461).

7

The Papal Record

In this era of ecumenism, many often overlook the abysmal record of the papacy. The Vatican has never repented of this. In May, 1990, the emperor of Japan publicly repented of the crimes perpetrated in Korea during the Japanese occupation of 1906-1945. But the papacy has never repented of her crimes of vastly greater proportions.

This summary of the papacy's record is not written in order to cause anyone to despise the Catholics because these people are greatly loved of God; however, in order to demonstrate why God, in His Word, uses such strong language in His denunciation of Catholicism, we need to understand that Scripture is speaking about the religious system, not against individual persons for whom He died.

We quote from a Catholic author lest Protestant sources are thought to be biased. Dr. Peter de Rosa (a former professor of ethics and metaphysics, in Westminster Seminary, and a former dean of theology, in Corpus Christi College) has not concealed this record in his classic work, *Vicars of Christ*.

Claiming to be in the apostolic succession from Peter, popes have led out in the most appalling evils. Who can seriously believe the claim of apostolic succession when popes have conducted themselves in a manner that is so foreign to the Christ-filled life of the apostle Peter? The Jews made similar claims, in their retort to Jesus, that they were the descendants of Abraham. This claim was genetically valid, but the character of these people proved how utterly false this claim was. The papal claim of apostolic succession is also a fallacy.

No one can successfully refute the fact that many evils were perpetrated, in the name of God, by the Roman Catholic Church. In 1432, a group of godly bishops held a council in Basel, Switzerland, without papal approval. These sincere prelates merely wished to cleanse the church of the more obvious evils in its midst. Their suggestions and the response of Pope Eugene IV typified papal responses over many years to such proposed reformations.

> In spite of curial efforts to scupper it, a council met in Basel in 1432. The bishops showed they were in earnest. [They declared that] from now on, all ecclesiastical appointments shall be made according to the canons of the Church; all simony[1] shall cease. From now on, all priests, from the highest to the lowest rank, shall put away their concubines. Whoever, within two months of this decree, neglects its demands shall be deprived of his office, though he be the bishop of Rome. From now on, the ecclesiastical administration of each country shall cease to depend upon papal caprice . . . The abuse of ban and

anathema by popes shall cease . . . From now on, the Roman curia [which are the popes] shall neither demand or receive any fees for ecclesiastical offices. From now on, a pope should think not of the world's treasures but only of those of the world to come.

This was strong meat. Too strong. The ruling pope, Eugene IV, summoned his own council at Florence. [The council that met in] Basel [in 1432] he labelled "a beggarly mob, mere vulgar fellows from the lowest dregs of the clergy, apostates, blaspheming rebels, men guilty of sacrilege, gaolbirds [jailbirds], men who without exception deserve only to be hunted back to the devil whence they come (Peter de Rosa, *Vicars of Christ*, p. 138).

One man who sought reformation and paid with his life as a result was the Bohemian Reformer, John Huss.

Huss, who was brave, chaste, incorruptible, a stern opponent of simony and clerical concubinage met a harsher fate. Forbidden counsel, tried on a trumped-up charge, interrogated by Dominicans who had not read his books, even in translation, he was sentenced to death . . . It was clearly more sinful to say, as did Huss and the New Testament, that, after the blessings the Eucharist should still be called "bread" than to be a greedy, murderous, incestuous pope who misled the church on almost everything (*ibid.*, pp. 132, 133).

This latter reference is to Pope John XXIII (no connection with the twentieth-century pope of the same name) who, the same year that Huss was martyred (1415), was deposed after his conviction on five charges. Peter de Rosa quotes Gibbons' record concerning the fact that the number of charges against Pope John XXIII was reduced from fifty-four to five.

> The most scandalous charges [against Pope John XXIII] were suppressed; the Vicar of Christ was only charged with piracy, murder, rape, sodomy, and incest (*ibid.*, p. 132).

For these crimes, the pope received a jail sentence of three years! It was said of the same pope that he was exonerated of the charge of heresy because he did not evince sufficient interest in religion to say anything heretical. Such secularization on the part of a Christian leader was shameful.

Even more shameful was the conduct of Pope Innocent IV and his curia who, because of a dispute with Emperor Frederick II, were forced to leave Rome and set up court in Lyons, France. After the emperor's death, Innocent IV and his entourage returned to Rome. History testifies that the pope was misnamed. In a letter that was dated 1520, Cardinal Hugo, writing in the pope's name, expressed appreciation to the citizens of Lyons for their hospitality during his period of dire need; however, the cardinal pointed out that all the benefits had not been one-sided was evidence of this fact.

> During our residence in your city, we [the curia] have been of very charitable assistance to you. On our arrival, we found scarcely three or four purchaseable sisters of love. Whilst at our departure we leave you, so to say, one brothel that extends from the western to the eastern gate (*ibid.*, p. 164).

No true Christian could experience anything but revulsion at this conduct by claimed religious leaders.

It is the iniquitous doctrine of papal infallibility that was proclaimed at the Vatican I Council of 1870 which prevents contemporary popes from expressing regret for these disgusting activities. One wonders what Guiseppe Sarto (better known as Pope Pius IX, who introduced the dogma of papal infallibility) thought about the statement that Pope Adrian VI made in 1523.

> If by the Roman Church you mean its head, or pontiff, it is without question that he can err even in matters touching the faith. He does this when he teaches heresy by his own judgment or decretal. In truth, many Roman pontiffs were heretics. The last of them was Pope John XII (*ibid.*, p. 285).

At the Vatican I Council, no less than 140 bishops absented themselves from this session which voted papal infallibility. They would have done themselves and their church a better service if they had displayed greater courage, and boldly voted what their consciences dictated. In the session, only two bishops evinced such courage—the Italian bishop, Riccio, of Cajazzo, and the American bishop Fitzgerald, of Little Rock; however, they also demonstrated the shallow depth of their convictions a few minutes later.

> Those two brave bishops, who, a moment ago, denied it, now confessed on their knees to Pius IX— "Modo credo, Sancte Pater"—that they believed it as sincerely and unreservedly as they believed in God's and Jesus' divinity. Theirs was the quickest conversion in history (*ibid.*, p. 187).

If, as had been declared, popes are infallible when they speak *ex cathedra*, then surely Pope Adrian VI's statement that popes have been fallible in matters of faith is an infallible statement. The reader will see at once the problem which is inherent in such a statement.

Applying the God-like quality of infallibility to some of history's most evil men underlines God's utter rejection of the papal system. It is a system which designates evils as virtues and virtues as evils.

> In his seventeenth-century book, *Romano Pontifice*, Cardinal Bellarmine stated, "If the pope were to err by imposing sins and forbidding virtues, the church would still have to consider sins as good and virtues as vices, or else she would sin against conscience" (*ibid.*, p. 71).

With such an abhorrent concept of right and wrong, one designed by the archdeceiver himself, no wonder Pope Clement XI (1700-1721) could declare the following:

> There is no higher duty than obedience to the pope. Obey him, and there can be no question of condemnation from God (*ibid.*, p. 325).

If this pope is to be believed, those who, at the command of the popes, perpetrated the Inquisition (in which millions of fruitful and innocent men and women were cruelly tortured and killed) were "pleasing" to our loving and beneficent God, the "justice" of the Inquisition, a part of papal policy for centuries, may be judged by the following:

> In the *Libro Nero* (Black Book) on display in the Vatican for the guidance of Inquisitors, as late as the end of the nineteenth century, it was stated, "Either the person confesses and he is proved guilty by his own confession, or he does not confess and is equally guilty on the evidence of witnesses. If a person confesses the whole of what he is accused of, he is unquestionably guilty of the whole; but, if he confesses only a part, he ought still to be regarded as guilty of the whole, since what he has confessed proves him to be capable of guilt as to the other points of the accusa-

tions . . . If, notwithstanding all the means employed, the unfortunate wretch still denies his guilt, he is to be considered as a victim of the devil. As such, he deserves no compassion from the servants of God nor the pity and indulgence of the Holy Mother Church. He is a son of perdition. Let him perish among the damned" (*ibid.*, p. 230).

[From the moment of arrest, the victim of the Inquisition] had no hope . . . Alone and friendless, he was refused legal representation . . . Defense witnesses were not allowed. All prosecution witnesses (their identities were kept secret from the prisoner) were given equal status. Among them might be the accuser's servants whom he had dismissed for theft or incompetence or others of ill-repute or unreliable testimony (*ibid.*, p. 231).

It is understandable why a Roman Catholic author was constrained to state Pope Innocent's opinion.

In [Pope] Innocent's view, it was more wicked for Albigenses to call him the antichrist than for him to prove it by burning them—men, women, and children by the thousands (Peter de Rosa, *Vicars of Christ*, p. 225).

Despite all this iniquity in the leadership of the Catholic Church, men today praise the papacy as a bastion of liberty, justice, and democracy. It must never be forgotten that, even today in the United States, there is an obvious difference between the privilages of democracy and the freedom of expression that individual Catholics enjoy in society and the secrecy and absolute control in church government.

A Catholic rejoices in openness, complete freedom of worship, and democracy. He takes it for granted that freedom leads to a deepening of the truth. He is used to his leaders having to present themselves for his approval. He can vote them in; he can vote them out. He demands press conferences, freedom of information, and an unfettered press that is like a second government. In the church, a Catholic has to put up with total secrecy and lack of accountability. There are no choices . . . He has to accept what he is given. In the church, there are no press conferences, no checks and balances, and no explanations. The control from the top is absolute. The impression given is that freedom and discussion lead to the dilution of truth (*Ibid.*, p. 209).

In truth, even in the last decade of the twentieth century, the papacy is the archopponent of liberty, justice, and democracy.

No wonder God is constrained to declare the final judgment of this corrupt religious body.

For her sins have reached unto heaven, and God hath remembered her iniquities. Reward her even as she rewarded you, and double unto her double according to her works: in the cup which she hath filled fill to her double. How, she hath glorified herself, and lived deliciously, so much torment and sorrow give her: for she saith in her heart, I sit a queen, and am no widow, and shall see no sorrow. Therefore shall her plagues come in one day, death, and mourning, and famine; and she shall be utterly burned with fire: for strong is the Lord God who judgeth her (Revelation 18:5-8).

Endnote

[1] The selling of church appointments.

8

The Deadly Wound Is Healed

The San Francisco *Chronicle*, Tuesday, February 12, 1929, exploded with the headlines, "Mussolini and Gasparri Sign Historic Roman Pact . . . Healed Wound of Many Years." It was hardly likely that the correspondent and the editors of the San Francisco *Chronicle* had any concept of the significance of the dramatic event that they were reporting. The previous day, February 11, 1929, Cardinal Gasparri (representing Pope Pius XI) and Benito Mussolini (representing King Victor Emmanuel III) signed the Lateran Treaty.

When the nation of Italy was reunited, in 1870, by Garibaldi, no temporal kingdom was allotted to the papacy. In fact, the Papal States were forcibly wrenched from Vatican control and ceded to the kingdom of Italy. This festering sore left a major rift between the Italian monarchy and the papacy. As a protest against the decision of the Italian monarchy to cede the Papal States to the kingdom of Italy, no pope had set foot outside the Vatican from 1870 to 1929; however, things changed with the signing of the Lateran Treaty. Among other things, the kingdom of Italy guaranteed the international sovereignty of the Holy See, giving it absolute and sole jurisdiction over the Vatican State. This territory was merely 108 acres. The words chosen for the San Francisco *Chronicle* report were most remarkable. These included "healed the wound of many years" and "healing the wound which had festered since 1870." These very words paralleled the words that were used in Scripture almost two thousand years before, in the prophecy, of the revival and renaissance of the papacy.

> And I saw one of his heads as it were wounded to death; and his *deadly wound was healed*: and all the world wondered after the beast (Revelation 13:3, emphasis added).

Revelation, chapter 13, provides dramatic insight into the final efforts of the antichrist power to deceive the world and coerce all its inhabitants to obey his edicts. It offers evidence that the papacy would dominate the Christian world for 1260 years. (See chapter 5, entitled "The Medieval Reign of the Papacy.") This period ended in 1798 when General Berthier, of Napoleon's army, conquered the various Italian states, and eventually took the reigning pope, Pius VI, prisoner to northern Italy and then back to southern France, where he died in August 1799. This act inflicted the deadly wound that was prophesied in Revelation 13:3. At that time, few foresaw the future revival of the papacy because of its complete destruction.

In the year 1797, the Directoire (revolutionary government of France) had commissioned Joseph Bonaparte (brother of Napoleon), who was already at Rome, to make plans that, upon the death of the sickly Pius VI, no new pope would be elected. The Directoire saw the papacy as the irreconcilable enemy of the French Republic. To the dismay of the French leadership, Pius VI survived and recovered from his illness. Had Pius VI died in 1797, as seemed certain, the prophecies of Daniel and Revelation, which told of the 1260-year medieval rule of the papacy, would have proven wrong by one year. Biblical prophecy is accurate to the very year.

On arrival in Rome in 1798, Berthier's officers demanded that Pope Pius VI surrender his temporal power. When he refused, he was dragged from the altar, his rings were removed from his fingers, and he was taken prisoner. With the death of Pius VI, in August 1799, and Napoleon's declared determination that no successor would be elected, it was almost universally believed that the papacy had come to its final and irreversible end. One correspondent wrote the obituary of the papacy.

However, the sure word of biblical prophecy said that the deadly wound would be healed (Revelation 13:3). That healing has been a long and slow process, but it began surprisingly early. Shortly after the death of Pius VI, the French Revolutionary forces had serious catastrophes, and troops had to be withdrawn from southern Italy. Taking advantage of this situation, the cardinals met and elected Barnabas Chiarominti as Pope Pius VII on March 14, 1800, only six and a half months after the pope's death; thus began the re-establishment of the papacy.

Surprisingly, Napoleon soon became reconciled to the fact that most of the French citizens supported the Roman Catholic Church. He signed a concordat with the Catholic Church, declaring that the state acknowledged the Catholic Church as the religion of France, and called for the loyalty of the bishops to the state. On December 2, 1804, reluctant Pope Pius VII had traveled to Paris in order to crown Napoleon as the emperor of France in Notre Dame Cathedral. Napoleon took the crown from the surprised pontiff and crowned himself as emperor. Today, the Vatican museum displays the magnificent pair of eight-feet-tall porcelain candlesticks that were used during the coronation ceremony which followed Napoleon's assumption of the title of emperor. Napoleon offered them as a gift to the restored papacy. Step by painful step, the papacy began its rise until the Lateran Treaty, of 1929, was signed. From this point onward, the power and influence of the papacy experienced steady growth. More recently, that growth has been dramatic.

It is strikingly significant that the deadly wound of modern spiritual Babylon parallels the wounding and resurgence of ancient Babylon. From the early time of the restoration of civilization after the Noachian flood, Babylon and Nineveh dominated the world. For at least 1,300 years, the city of Babylon had held the pride of the Middle East. This period of time was very similar to the 1260 years of papal domination in medieval Europe; however, in the year 700 B.C., ancient Babylon was to receive its deadly wound. At this time, Assyria (to the northwest) had assumed domination over Babylon. Just as France held similar religious beliefs to Italy, so Assyria had held similar pagan concepts to those of Babylon.

In 721 B.C., Sargon II completed the captivity of the Israelites that was commenced by his predecessor, Shalmaneser V. After the death of Sargon II in 705, Sennacherib cast his eyes upon the southern kingdom of Judah. Marshaling a mighty army, Sennacherib would have succeeded, but the miraculous intervention of God left 185,000 Assyrian soldiers dead outside the walls of Jerusalem. (See 2 Chronicles, chapter 32.)

After the death of so many soldiers, the army of Sennacherib was depleted. Sensing the weakness of Assyria, the Babylonians revolted; however, Sennacherib succeeded in putting together another army that ruthlessly put down the revolt of the Babylonians, destroyed multitudes of its people and its images, and razed the city to the ground. This seemed to be the final demise of ancient Babylon. It had received a deadly wound.

Before the end of the seventh century B.C., Nabopolassar, the Chaldean, assumed the throne of Babylon. He destroyed Nineveh, and established a kingdom that was greater than any before. Under his son, Nebuchadnezzar, the Neo-Babylonian Empire became the greatest in the world. And the city of Babylon was established as the center of culture and education. The deadly wound certainly was healed; yet the prophet, Jeremiah, accurately prophesied the events which were to occur during the height of its power.

Out of the north there cometh up a nation
against her, which shall make her land desolate, and
none shall dwell therein: they shall remove, they shall
depart, both man and beast (Jeremiah 50:3).

Come against her from the utmost border, open her
storehouses: cast her up as heaps, and destroy her utterly: let nothing of her be left (Jeremiah 50:26).

Therefore the wild beasts of the desert with the
wild beasts of the islands shall dwell there, and the
owls shall dwell therein: and it shall be no more in-
habited for ever; neither shall it be dwelt in from
generation to generation. As God overthrew Sodom
and Gomorrah and the neighbour cities thereof, saith
the Lord; so shall no man abide there, neither shall
any son of man dwell therein (Jeremiah 50:39, 40).

And will send unto Babylon fanners, that shall fan
her, and shall empty her land: for in the day of trouble
they shall be against her round about (Jeremiah 51:2).

And the land shall tremble and sorrow: for every
purpose of the Lord shall be performed against
Babylon, to make the land of Babylon a desolation
without an inhabitant (Jeremiah 51:29).

Subsequent to the dramatic healing of the deadly wound
of ancient Babylon, the city was destroyed at the height of
its glory and power, by Medo-Persia, in 539 B.C. In an
amazing parallel, the Bible foretells the wounding, restoration, and final destruction of modern Babylon at the height
of its glory and power.

And there followed another angel, saying, Babylon
is fallen, is fallen, that great city, because she made all
nations drink of the wine of the wrath of her fornica-
tion. And the third angel followed them, saying with a
loud voice, If any man worship the beast and his
image, and receive his mark in his forehead, or in his

hand, the same shall drink of the wine of the wrath of God, which is poured out without mixture into the cup of his indignation; and he shall be tormented with fire and brimstone in the presence of the holy angels, and in the presence of the Lamb: and the smoke of their torment ascendeth up for ever and ever: and they have no rest day or night, who worship the beast and his image, and whosoever receiveth the mark of his name (Revelation 14:8-11).

And the great city was divided into three parts, and the cities of the nations fell: and great Babylon came in remembrance before God, to give unto her the cup of the wine of the fierceness of his wrath (Revelation 16:19).

We are living during the time that the papacy is being restored to even greater power than it exercised during the Middle Ages. The influence of the medieval papacy was, for the most part, confined to the sphere of Europe; however, the neo-papal power is asserting its mighty influence over the whole earth.

And all the world wondered after the beast (Revelation 13:3).

And all that dwell upon the earth shall worship him, whose names are not written in the book of life of the Lamb slain from the foundation of the world (Revelation 13:8).

And the woman which thou sawest is that great city, which reigneth over the kings of the earth (Revelation 17:18).

As lads growing up, we well-remember Pope Pius XII (successor to Pius XI). As Cardinal Pacelli, he had been papal nuncio to Nazi Germany. He was greatly suspicioned, during World War II, of being sympathetic to the Nazi and Fascist causes. It was still an era of contention between many Protestants and Roman Catholics. We cannot forget our maternal grandfather, John Bailey (of northern Irish Protestant heritage), and his unwavering bigotry against Roman Catholics. He was an avid reader of *The Rock*, a weekly paper put out by anti-Catholic Protestants who reported every excess of the Roman Catholic Church.

Many years later, Russell (then a physician in Sydney) happened to have the editor of *The Rock*, Mr. Campbell, as his patient. Russell mentioned our grandfather's loyalty to his paper. The editor bitterly reported that, in the 1940s, this paper had a weekly circulation of 40,000 copies, but had dropped, by the 1970s, to a monthly paper with a circulation of about 2,000. Then, with strong emotion, he added, "It's all the fault of those ecumaniacs." Times had certainly changed.

The suspicion that Pope Pius XII engendered was especially strong in the allied nations. At that time, it was easy to distrust the papacy and the Roman Catholic Church. After the death of Pius XII, in 1958, the College of Cardinals unexpectedly chose the 76-year-old Cardinal Roncalli as Pope John XXIII. Many expressed the view that he would be an interim pope until the cardinals could agree upon a more suitable younger man. But John XXIII, in four and a half short years, changed the face of Catholicism. His Vatican II Council altered the image of the papacy from one of intrigue and suspicion to that of love and social justice. The impact of this change was more obvious in the United States than in most countries. Just prior to the Lateran Treaty, Al Smith had accepted the Democratic nomination as the 1928 presidential candidate. But Smith, a Roman Catholic, was overwhelmingly defeated by the Republican, Herbert Hoover. Anti-Catholic feelings clearly governed the voters' decision at that time. Some predicted that no major party would be foolish enough to again field a Roman Catholic presidential candidate.

Little more than 30 years later, the ecumenical climate was so favorable and Pope John XXIII had so modified the papal image that John Kennedy, a Roman Catholic, not only received his party's endorsement but won the presidency. Since then, the relationship between the papacy and Washington has shown dramatic improvement. American presidents now commonly visit the pope. In the 1980s, Protestant Ronald Reagan utilized the growing popularity of the papacy to his political advantage. He correctly perceived that he could enhance his reelection prospects by meeting with Pope John Paul II, in Fairbanks, Alaska, in 1984. A few decades earlier, such a meeting would have almost certainly doomed his reelection prospects; further, President Reagan engendered remarkably little opposition to his move to reestablish full diplomatic relations with the papacy for the first time since the 1860s.

In the latter part of the 1980s, we witnessed even greater evidences of the revival of papal influence. For decades, the relentless advances of atheistic communism, which had engulfed almost half the population of the world, had seemed like an irresistible force that threatened to envelope the whole planet. Communism's advances were so spectacular that most overlooked the steady resurgence of the papacy. Only those who continued to diligently search the sure Word of scriptural prophecy were not deluded. They were brave enough to declare that it was not communism but Catholicism that would be the major "player" in the events that would culminate in the return of Jesus.

The latter part of the 1980s left the world spellbound with the rapidity of the changes which occurred in both the political and religious worlds. As communism was being dismantled in Eastern Europe, the religious world was relentlessly pursuing union, not only among Protestant denominations but, even more significantly, between Catholics and Protestants. (See chapter 9, entitled "And All That Dwell Upon the Earth Shall Worship Him.") The stage was being set for the great final test of loyalty to God.

9

All That Dwell Upon the Earth Shall Worship Him

In the religious world, the ecumenical movement is gaining great momentum. Emphasis is placed upon both organic union and spiritual union. An organic union is the physical union of two or more churches into a single church body. Many such unions have already been formed, including the United Methodist Church of America, the United Church of Canada, the Uniting Church of Australia, and the Church of South India. Well-known church leaders indicate that they will not be satisfied until all Christian churches are united into one body.

Of course, this goal has many impelling aspects. The United Christian Church, it is believed, will present a wonderful power to modern Christianity and the non-Christian world in the most persuasive manner; however, an examination of almost all uniting churches reveals signs of impotency, membership loss, and stagnation.

It is not hard to understand the reason for the failure of the architects of these united churches to fulfill their expectations. In 1986, Colin attended the sixth International Congress for the Prevention of Alcoholism and Drug Dependencies that was held in Nice, France. At the banquet which was held at the conclusion of the congress, he was seated next to a minister of the Uniting Church of Australia. During their conversation, Colin inquired concerning the nature of the doctrinal agreements that the Methodists, Presbyterians, and Congregationalists (who formed the Uniting Church) had made. The clergyman asserted that they united on New Testament Christianity, not on doctrine. Pressing the issue a little further, Colin asked, "What common basis did the freewill Methodists find for unity with predestinarian Presbyterians?" The minister admitted that he had never given thought to the issue, although he had been a Methodist minister before this union took place. Later, he sent Colin a copy of the articles of Uniting. A review of these articles did not reveal one single belief upon which the consolidated church had been established.

In 1977, Russell had had a similar experience. As Deputy Medical Superintendent of the Austin Hospital, in Melbourne, he supervised the chaplaincy. Graham Gibbens, a Presbyterian minister, was the senior chaplain. When asked concerning the major doctrinal difference between Presbyterians and Methodists, in relation to their proposed union in that year, Graham replied, "You know, I've never given it any thought." One wonders how John Knox (founder of the Presbyterian Church), John Wesley (founder of the Methodist Church), and the nonconformists of England (who established the Congregationalist Church) would have reacted to this careless attitude toward biblical doctrine.

The ecumenical movement and the World Council of Churches have determined to de-emphasize doctrine. Many have naively accepted the proposition that "it is not doctrine we need, but Christ," without realizing that every doctrine of the Scriptures is a dynamic revelation of Christ. How can one preach the doctrine of the Incarnation without including the Babe of Bethlehem who became man's Redeemer? How can one preach concerning the fate of man in death without preaching of the One who is the Resurrection and the Life? How can one preach baptism outside the context of the One who renews His life to us? How can one preach about the heavenly high priestly ministry of Christ without preaching about the One who is our Sacrifice, Judge, High Priest, Mediator, Advocate, and Intercessor? How can one preach the law of God without revealing the One who is the very transcript of His character? With the exception of truth and doctrine, our faith is empty; and our knowledge of Christ is minimal. A new nondoctrinal approach to religion leaves the adherents weak, ignorant, uncertain, and an easy prey for the archdeceiver.

Surely, the ecumenical movement is a device of the enemy of souls to prepare a people to be partners in the eternal, destructive "game" of Satan instead of rising to shine for Christ. In the year 1989, leading Christian representatives made some remarkable pronouncements. After his visit with the pope, Robert Runcie, archbishop of Canterbury and primate in the Anglican Church in Great

Britain, on October 2, 1989, urged all Christians to recognize the pope as the leader of all Christians.

> Archbishop Robert Runcie, the head of the Anglican Church who is discussing unification with the Roman Catholic Church, called for Christians to accept the pope as the common leader, presiding in love (Charlottesville, Virginia, *Daily Progress*, Oct. 1, 1989).

This call was not given without protest from a small vocal group of determined Protestants.

> Robert Runcie suggested, at the weekend in Rome, that Christians throughout the world should accept the pope as universal primate. This has aroused Protestant anger (Singapore *Straits Times*, Oct. 3, 1989).

Many are confidently predicting the reunification of the two largest churches in the world, the Church of England and the Church of Rome, by the year 2000. If this happens, the Reformation will have come a full circle. The Anglo-Catholic movement within the Church of England, which began in the 1820s at Oxford University, will finally have triumphed.

This is so significant because Bible prophecy predicted that, at the end-time, almost everyone in the world will give allegiance to the papacy. John referred to the papacy, using the symbol of the beast.

> And I saw one of his heads as it were wounded to death; and his deadly wound was healed: and *all the world wondered after the beast* (Revelation 13:3, emphasis added).

> And all that dwell upon the earth shall worship him, whose names are not written in the book of life

of the Lamb slain from the foundation of the world
(Revelation 13:8).

The beast that thou sawest was, and is not; and
shall ascend out of the bottomless pit, and go into perdition: and they that dwell on the earth shall wonder,
whose names were not written in the book of life from
the foundation of the world, when they behold the
beast that was, and is not, and yet is (Revelation 17:8).

Mainline Protestantism in the United States, including
Presbyterians, Congregationalists, Methodists, Lutherans,
and Episcopalians, are the controlling backbone of
American society and politics, and has experienced strong
reversal in the last 30 years. *Time* magazine, May 22,
1989, reported that, since 1965, the United Church of Christ
(Congregationalists) had shrunk 20 percent; Presbyterians,
25 percent; the Episcopal Church, 28 percent; Methodists,
18 percent; and the Christian Church (Disciples of Christ),
43 percent. Together, they had a net loss of 5.2 million
members. The growth of American Roman Catholics, 16
percent in the same period, is quite significant.

Time magazine also reports that Sunday School participa-
tion in the mainline churches has dropped 55 percent in the
past two decades. This woeful omen is most frightening for
these mainline Protestant churches who were once the
powerful standard makers of American society. The quote
from Professor Richard Mouw, of the nondenominational
Fuller Theological Seminary, in California, is the most
striking statement from the article: "If there is an establishment voice today, it is that of Roman Catholicism. The
Catholics are the calm, dignified, authoritative voices."
Richard John Neuhaus supports this view, in a book he

authored which claims that this is the *Catholic moment* in America.

The report of the 10-year dialogue between Roman Catholic theologians and theologians who represent the Southern Baptist Conference (the two largest churches in the United States) is even more significant than reports of the events within the Church of England and mainline Protestant churches in the United States. The Associated Press reported what the joint communique stated.

> We not only confessed, but experienced *one Lord, one Faith, and one Baptism* (*Williamson Daily News*, Aug. 26, 1989, emphasis added).

It is impossible to imagine how Southern Baptist theologians could experience one Lord with a church that claims that the pope is another God on earth. It is certainly impossible to understand how a church which has so strongly proclaimed salvation by faith can confess to have spiritual union in faith with a church that has steadfastly adhered to salvation by faith *and* works (the keeping of the seven sacred sacraments). Finally, we are puzzled about how a church which practices adult baptism by immersion could compromise this one baptism with Roman Catholics who practice infant sprinkling, because the sprinkling of infants is a satanic counterfeit of true baptism. How could Southern Baptist theologians so pervert the faith of their Fathers?

The newspaper further reported that "the Southern Baptists and Roman Catholics . . . generally have been regarded as doctrinally far apart, but their scholars find that they basically agree" (*ibid.*). Here we can discern the peril of entrusting doctrinal decisions to a few theologians or scholars. Every conceivable perversion of truth has found support, in some way or another, from the scholars. There is hardly a theological training school throughout the world that is committed to the teaching of the pure faith of Jesus. As in Jesus' day, it is the common folk who value pure biblical truth; and the oracles of God have been entrusted to them.

> The wayfaring men, though fools, shall not err therein (Isaiah 35:8).

The missionary endeavors of the future will be quite significantly hindered if the report's following statement is excepted.

> Both sides admitted past unfairness to each other, with predominantly Roman Catholic countries discriminating against Southern Baptist missionaries, and the latter laboring among Catholics without respecting their faith. Such *competition and conflict in missionary work* can become a stumbling block to those who have not heard the gospel (*Williamson Daily News*, Aug. 26, 1989, emphasis added).

Undoubtedly, many sincere Southern Baptists will be alarmed by this report. Evangelical Anglicans are also deeply concerned by the plea of Archbishop Runcie for closer ties with the papacy. But, in these actions, the discerning Christian will see that the time has come when all Christians who do not give supreme homage to Christ and the Bible will eventually give their allegiance to the papacy; thus this fulfills the unerring prophecy that all the world will wonder after the beast (Revelation 13:3). While a casual perusal of this joint declaration may seem good in many ways, it will basically lead the Southern Baptists to

diminish and ultimately eliminate all work for the salvation of Catholic Church members; thus Southern Baptists
cannot give that final call, by God's elect, to His precious
saints who are still members of the Roman Catholic
Church.

> And I heard another voice from heaven, saying,
> *Come out of her, my people,* that ye be not partakers of
> her sins, and that ye receive not of her plagues. For
> her sins have reached unto heaven, and God hath
> remembered her iniquities (Revelation 18:4, 5, em-
> phasis added).

U.S. News and World Report magazine, January 15, 1990,
addressed another new phenomenon in the United States—
the growing trend of Protestants, even Evangelicals, to
move toward liturgical ritualistic, ceremonial, and
sacramental forms of religion. This movement apparently
is a reaction against the informal, often irreverent, forms of
worship that have arisen out of the Pentecostal and Charis-
matic movements. Ritualistic worship has appealed to
some who are weary of listening to tame, bland sermons of
repetitious themes in many mainline churches. The rituals
of the Orthodox churches have often been practiced as a
refreshing alternative. Such a movement will surely be able
to accommodate itself to the Roman Catholic form of
sacramentalism.

This thrust toward one world religion envisages the en-
compassment of far more sects than Christendom. In 1988,
Dr. Robert Runcie gave the Sir Francis Younghusband
Memorial Lecture at Lambeth Palace (home of the
archbishop of Canterbury) for the fiftieth anniversary of
the establishment of the World Congress of Faiths. He

ominously quoted the words of the late Sir Francis: "All the centuries that the Spirit of God has been working in Christians, He must also have been working in Hindus, Buddhists, Muslims, and others." Dr. Runcie then commented that dialogue enabled people of various religions "to share the sustaining insights and transforming treasures of their faith, and to recognize an affinity of the human heart in the fellowship of the Spirit." The archbishop's reflection on a visit to India was even more disconcerting.

> . . . *[He arrived with] the certainties of an encapsulated Western Christianity* but came away realizing that there are *new ways of thinking about God, Christ, and the world.* He spoke of his experience of God among the Hindus of Madras, "where gods and goddesses take hundreds of different forms and images. The sheer diversity of the Divine was disconcerting. God somehow seemed greater than Western monism . . . We have lost something that other faiths may help to restore to us" (*The Sentinel,* vol. 42, No. 4, spring 1989, emphasis added).

Those who do not accept God's commission to urge Christians to forsake apostate religions will themselves be found among that huge ecumenical group who receive the seven last plagues that are cited in Revelation 16. Myriads of formal Christians will be lost in spiritual Babylon. But God will have a remnant who will give God's final invitation to the world.

> And the dragon was wroth with the woman, and went to make war with the remnant of her seed, which keep the commandments of God, and have the testimony of Jesus Christ (Revelation 12:17).

This page intentionally left blank.

10

Globalism and One World Government

Just as unity movements are gathering strength within Christendom, so the tide of unity in the political world is swelling. The concepts of a one world government and globalism have much support. Contrary to the views of many, this is a most serious movement. Many political philosophers believe that a single would government is the only hope for the survival of the human race. Large numbers of politicians in developing countries are also attracted to to this concept, believing that such unity is economically benificial to humanity. Many of the most avid advocates of political unity have made extravagant claims about the advantages of a one world government. The claim that such a government will eliminate poverty and starvation and establish a new order where all would share in the resources of the affluent nations of the world is particularly attractive to those in developing countries. This is a pipedream; but it is held by those who are blind to the reality of the abject poverty that is still in most first world countries, including the United States.

Passivists are also attracted to the concept of a one-world government, believing that a world that is united under one government will provide a peaceful environment. But people of this persuasion ignore the fact that civil war is presently more common than international war.

Satan, in his last desperate effort to control the world, is striving to gather churches and governments under his banner. This greatly facilitates his efforts to gain total control of the world. Using his talents, honed by millennia of experimentation with the human mind, he now is making his final effort to capture the total allegiance of the human race.

> Woe to the inhabiters of the earth and of the sea! for the devil is come down unto you, having great wrath, because he knoweth that he hath but a short time (Revelation 12:12).

> Be sober, be vigilant; because your adversary the devil, as a roaring lion, walketh about, seeking whom he may devour (1 Peter 5:8).

> And the dragon was wroth with the woman, and went to make war with the remnant of her seed, which keep the commandments of God, and have the testimony of Jesus Christ (Revelation 12:17).

> For there shall arise false Christs, and false prophets, and shall shew great signs and wonders; insomuch that, if it were possible, they shall deceive the very elect (Matthew 24:24).

The present thrust for political unity is not unique. By conquest, men such as Charlemagne, Napoleon, Kaiser Wilhelm, and Hitler have tried to unite Europe, as well as the world. The medieval church attempted to achieve unity built upon a common faith. It established the Holy Roman Empire, but it has frequently been said that, "it was neither holy, Roman, nor was it an empire." In the aftermath of the Napoleonic wars, the Austrian, Prince Klemens Metternich-Winneburg, hoped to bring peace by an agreement that would secure the borders of European nations where they were.

After the Metternich system, as it was called, broke down during the revolutions of 1848, Queen Victoria chose to encourage the intermarriage of all the royal families of Europe. She succeeded in this, but, in bringing peace, she did not. The stark reality of this was witnessed in World War I when King George V, of Great Britain, was leading his nation against his first cousin, Kaiser Wilhelm of Germany. The word of prophecy had proclaimed that the reunification of Europe will not take place.

The prophet, Daniel (see Daniel, chapter 2), told about the rise of four great powers that were represented by the great image. The first was the head of gold that represented the kingdom of Babylon; then followed the silver arms and breast of Medo-Persia; succeeded by the brass of Greece, and the iron of Rome. The prophecy finally presented the mixture of iron and clay in the ten toes of the image. This symbol represented the division of the Roman Empire into ten European kingdoms. This division was completed by A.D. 476.

> And as the toes of the feet were part of iron, and part of clay, so the kingdom shall be partly strong, and partly broken. And whereas thou sawest iron mixed with miry clay, they shall mingle themselves

with the seed of men: but they shall not cleave one to
another, even as iron is not mixed with clay (Daniel
2:42, 43).

Human efforts to unite Europe have consistently failed,
as the prophecy declared; however, a new effort is being
made to unite Europe through economic ties. There is no
doubt that the architects of the European Economic Community (EEC, often known as the Common Market) had
goals far beyond economic unity leading to political unity.
The EEC had its beginnings in 1957. The initial gathering,
in the City Hall of Rome, was sealed by what is significantly known as the Treaty of Rome. Initially, six nations were
signatories to the treaty—West Germany, France, Italy,
Holland, Belgium, and Luxembourg. Subsequently, six
more nations have joined—Great Britain, the Irish
Republic, Spain, Portugal, Denmark, and Greece.

Together, these nations represent an economic output
that exceeds that of the United States. They now have a
European parliament that is situated in Strasbourg. While
much of the role of the parliament is advisory, it has attracted some notable deputies, such as Willy Brandt who
was former chancellor of West Germany. Many see its future role as one of increasing political influence. Its powerful influence was demonstrated in June 1989, when
Margaret Thatcher's Conservative Party, in Great Britain,
took a sound beating at the hands of the Opposition
Labour Party in the election of deputies to the European
parliament. This greatly weakened the prime minister's efforts to modify the agreements on the European monetary
system that is scheduled for 1992. When, in the week following the elections, she was in Spain with the leaders of

the other 11 nations, she found herself almost impotent to make headway in her efforts.

The year 1992 will be an important year for the EEC. That is the date set for the introduction of the European monetary system (EMS). The plan is to introduce the Eurodollar. It is hard to imagine how this new system will take over the British pound, the Danish kroner, the Dutch guilder, the French franc, the West German mark, the Spanish peso, the Italian lira, and the Greek drachma. In that year, it is planned that all border controls between member nations will disappear. In fact, some controls have already been removed.

In 1987, Colin was driven from Holland to Belgium. He discovered that there were no immigration or customs barriers between the two countries. After 1992, once a citizen of a country that is outside the EEC arrives at an entry point in any one of the 12 nations, he will not need any further entry formalities in order to cross national borders. National passports in member countries of the EEC have already been abolished, and all citizens of the 12 nations receive a common European passport.

It is not difficult to understand how this European movement fits into the final plans of Satan. John, the revelator, foresaw the time when the papal power would implement an economic boycott against God's faithful people.

> And that no man might buy or sell, save he that
> had the mark, or the name of the beast, or the number
> of his name (Revelation 13:17).

A united Europe could easily facilitate this boycott, particularly a union that is primarily based upon economic principles. The remarkable events of contemporary history urge us to realize the fact that the end of the world is near. While Europe will not unite into a single nation, it is clear that the ties will become so close that, more and more, the papacy will be in a strong position to exert a controlling influence over the united community of European nations. These united powers will indeed provide the human strength to enforce the dictates of the papacy.

> And the ten horns which thou sawest are ten kings, which have received no kingdom as yet; but receive power as kings one hour with the beast. These have one mind, and shall give their power and strength unto the beast (Revelation 17:12, 13).

The Eastern European nations are already turning to the pope and the Vatican for guidance. In a poll that was conducted toward the end of 1989 in Poland, 87 percent of those who voted said that they trusted the Roman Catholic Church; and only 11 percent had said that they had confidence in the Communist Party (San Francisco *Chronicle*, Nov. 16, 1989). Tadewsz Mazowiecki, solidarity president of Poland, made his first international visit with the pope. It might be argued that, like the pope, he is Polish and Catholic, but, this in itself represents an important change from the approach of the former communist leaders. Diplomatic relations between the Vatican and Poland were quickly normalized. Later in the year, Catholic representatives from Hungary visited the Vatican in order to dialogue on church and state relations. There is no doubt that these once hard-line communist nations are now turning to the papacy for guidance and support.

> And I saw one of his heads as it were wounded to
> death; and his deadly wound was healed: and *all the
> world wondered after the beast* (Revelation 13:3, em-
> phasis added).

The recent events in Eastern Europe provide amazing
evidence of the failure of the communist party to destroy
religion. It is clear that religion has flourished much more
under communist repression than under Western freedom.
During December 1989, the Lithuanians of the Soviet
Union exercised a newfound religious freedom for the estimated 3,000,000 Catholics among its 3,600,000 population.

The most significant event of December 1989 was not the
summit meeting of President George Bush with Mikhail
Gorbachev; instead, it was Gorbachev's unprecedented
visit to the Vatican. The Washington *Post* of December 2,
1989, made this striking statement:

> Of all the meetings with world leaders that Gor-
> bachev has had since he became the Communist Party
> general secretary in March 1985, today's [with Pope
> John Paul II] was probably the most extraordinary
> (Washington *Post* of Dec. 2, 1982).

Time magazine emphasized the significance of the meeting with these words:

> More than any of the 18 summit meetings between
> Soviet leaders and U.S. presidents, Gorbachev's
> pilgrimage to the papal library will make his nation a
> respectable participant in world discourse (*Time*
> magazine, Australian edition, Dec. 4, 1989).

Gorbachev himself described the visit as "a truly extraordinary event," and it certainly was because no general
secretary of the Soviet Union had visited the reigning pope
since the arrival of Communism in Russia more than seven

decades ago. In the same Washington *Post* report, the
pope was quoted as saying that the meeting was "a sign of
the times that have slowly matured, a sign that is rich in
promise." Prophecy-studying Christians will see great significance, especially in the last portion of that statement.

At the meeting with Gorbachev, the pope had a heavy
burden upon his mind—the fate of the Ukrainian Catholics.
In the 1940s, Stalin had almost destroyed the Ukrainian
Catholic Church (between four and five million members),
disbanded its organization, and forced them to unite with
the Russian Orthodox Church. This group became the
largest persecuted group of Christians in the world.

When invited to visit Moscow, John Paul II stipulated
that he could accept Gorbachev's invitation only if permission was granted him to first visit the Lithuanian and Ukrainian Catholics, and only when the Ukrainian Catholic
Church was allowed to reorganize and function normally.
Gorbachev agreed to hasten this event. Just prior to the
meeting that was held between Gorbachev and the pope, a
Roman Catholic priest was interviewed on an American
CBS news feature. His significant statement was that "the
meeting is between the lion and the lamb, but no one is
sure which one is the lion and which is the lamb." The
meeting itself quickly showed that it was the pope who
held the upper hand. He was, without question, the lion.

We can expect these events to continue in rapid succession. It is certain that before this book is published, many
additional events will show the dominant role of the
papacy in world religion and political events. Truly, the
world is "wondering after the beast." Soon only those who

have their names written in the Lamb's book of life will refuse to worship him. Unquestionably, this is a time for all of God's people to draw closer to their Saviour. It is a time to look up, for our redemption draweth nigh (Luke 21:28). This is a time when every faithful servant of Christ must make his calling and election sure (2 Peter 1:10).

This page intentionally left blank.

11

European Political Unity

$\mathbf{A}$t the end of April 1990, the 12 nations of the European Economic Community met in Dublin, the Republic of Ireland, in conference. Flushed with the euphoria which had arisen over the imminent unity of East and West Germany, the West German chancellor, Helmut Kohl, together with the French president, Francois Mitterrand, urged the members of the community to work toward political integration (Singapore *Straits Times*, April 30, 1990).

Prime Minister Charles Haughey, of Ireland, who was then the president of the European Economic Community (a post which rotates every six months among the heads of the 12 member states), had called this special meeting to discuss the matter of German unity. Taking advantage of this extraordinary session, Kohl and Mitterrand made a proposal to extend the meeting to discuss European political unity. The Franco-Germans expressed themselves in this letter:

> Given the profound changes in Europe, the estab-
> lishment of the EC internal market and the realization
> of economic and monetary union, we believe it is
> necessary to accelerate the political construction of the
> 12 (*ibid.*, April 21, 1990).

These leaders left no doubt concerning the time frame
that they envisaged:

> Our objective is that these fundamental reforms—
> economic and monetary union as well as political
> union—take effect on January 1, 1993, after the
> ratification by national parliaments (*ibid.*).

It should not pass unnoticed that the two leaders
referred to the European Economic Community, not as the
EEC, but as the EC—the European Community. The latter
abbreviation is growing in popularity as the emphasis for
European unity is changing from a purely economic union
to one of political significance.

Ever since the destruction of Imperial Rome, one con-
queror after another has entertained ambitions to unite
Europe under his authority. Men such as Charlemange,
Napoleon Bonaparte, Kaiser Wilhelm, and Adolf Hitler
have pursued this delusion of grandeur, but each has
decidedly failed in reaching his ambition.

Now we see, for the first time, an effort to unite
European nations by peaceful means, simply relying upon
their acquiescence. This initiative of Chancellor Kohl and
President Mitterrand is doomed to fail just as surely as did
the efforts of dictators to achieve this aim by conquests.
God's mighty Word has spoken! In one of the great
prophecies of Scripture, God outlined the history of the
world from the days of Nebuchadnezzar, king of Babylon,

until the second coming of Christ. This vast stretch of prophetic time was viewed in a symbolic dream by King Nebuchadnezzar himself. In this dream, he saw a statue composed of a head of gold which represented his own kingdom of Babylon. This was followed by the chest and arms of silver that represented the Medo-Persian Empire which succeeded Babylon. The third portion of the statue consisted of an abdomen and thighs of bronze, which represented the Grecian Empire. This was followed by the legs of iron which represented the mighty Roman Empire that succeeded Greece.

But it is the feet which interest us today. Unlike the rest of the image's body, these feet were not composed of metal alone, as Scripture tells us.

> His legs of iron, his feet part of iron and part of clay (Daniel 2:33).

The Bible makes it perfectly plain that the iron kingdom of Rome would eventually be divided into the various nations of Europe; furthermore, in the history of this world, these nations would never again unite.

> And whereas thou sawest the feet and toes, part of potters' clay, and part of iron, the kingdom shall be divided; but there shall be in it of the strength of the iron, forasmuch as thou sawest the iron mixed with the miry clay. And as the toes of the feet were part of iron, and part of clay, so the kingdom shall be partly strong and partly broken. And whereas thou sawest the iron mixed with miry clay, they shall mingle themselves with the seed of men: but they shall not cleave one to another, even as iron is not mixed with clay (Daniel 2:41-43).

John the revelator spoke of the day when the ten horns
(or the ten toes as they are depicted in Daniel) would represent the nations of Europe that would "have one mind"
(Revelation 17:13). This is certainly not referring to political unity. It refers to unity in purpose. The prophecy of
Daniel 2 reveals that the nations of Europe would never
again unite as a single political entity—"They shall not
cleave one to another." While we can look for unanimity of
purpose among the nations of Europe, particularly in their
support for papal dominance, we can be just as certain that
these nations will not politically unite again.

It is very likely that Francois Mitterrand, in supporting
the German proposal, was motivated by the fear of a
united Germany.

France has suffered three German occupations in the last
120 years. The French people no doubt believe that, in a
united Europe, they would have much more security
against a revitalized Germany than they have experienced
in the past; however, in this, they are doomed to disap-
pointment. While it is true that Mrs. Thatcher is a particularly strong opponent of the European political unity,
she, nevertheless, correctly predicted that "the process of
European union would founder as soon as member states
faced the prospect of having to cede national sovereignty
and accept collective decision making" (Singapore *Straits
Times*, April 1990).

We must not overlook the fact that France is a Catholic
nation and that Chancellor Kohl leads the Catholic political
party of Germany. Make no mistake, the Vatican is carefully monitoring, if not actively instigating, the move for a

united Europe. Pope John Paul II has called "an unprecedented Europe-wide meeting of bishops to discuss spread-
ing the church's message across the continent" (*ibid.*, April
23, 1990).

Let us notice this fact in the light of the call from France
and Germany, a few days later, for European unity. The interest of the Roman Catholic Church in European unity is
as intense as it is self-serving.

> The concept of a united Europe, one that recognizes
> its Christian roots, has been an important thread run-
> ning through the pope's speeches on a two-day visit
> to Czechoslovakia. . . . Europe has about 1,000 of the
> world's 3,000 bishops. The synod apparently will for-
> mulate a strategy to meet the pope's vision of a
> Europe united by its Christian roots (*ibid.*).

We may rest assured that what the pope means by Christian roots is *Roman Catholic* roots; thus Kohl and Mitterrand, in their letter to Prime Minister Haughey, were
either reflecting the pope's wishes or they were using their
good offices, at the request of the pope, to forward his
desires.

For countries such as France and Germany, which are
likely to dominate any united Europe, there would be
potential advantages. But what about the fate of the
smaller countries? Already, it is reported that Mrs.
Thatcher was not alone in her stand against political union.

> Community leaders said other countries such as
> Denmark, Luxembourg, and Portugal also had reser-
> vations (*ibid.*).

It is understandable that smaller nations such as Denmark, Luxembourg, and Portugal would be very hesitant

to join a united states of Europe. The Union of Soviet
Socialist Republics has provided a contemporary example
of the difficulty of ruling a nation of united states that consists of concentrations of diverse ethnic citizens. We only
have to examine the situations in the Baltic states and the
states of Armenia, Georgia, and Azerbaijan in order to
realize that the fate of ethnic minorities within a larger
union is not to be desired.

If the smaller countries of Europe were to lose their
sovereignty, they would become mere puppets in the
hands of the larger nations. This would be particularly so
if all of Europe was united to include the U.S.S.R., Britain,
France, and Germany.

Undoubtedly, calls for a united Europe will continue, but
we have the sure Word of God that political union in
Europe will not transpire. No student of God's Word
could ever doubt this fact. There will be, as we have mentioned, a coming together of these nations in purpose and
ideals that are particularly related to the religious issues
and the dominance of the Vatican in these religious issues.
But that unity will transpire despite the fact that national
sovereignties will be maintained. The European parliament will never become a sovereign parliament for a single
nation—the united states of Europe—because God, in His
infallible foreknowledge, has revealed that this will never
transpire.

We are living in the last days. Satan is diligent in his attempts to make of none effect the prophecies of God. He,
too, is doomed to failure. We are near the end of this
world's history. Speaking of the division of Europe, God

has revealed to us what will follow the period of the divided nations of Europe.

> And in the days of these kings shall the God of heaven set up a kingdom, that shall never be destroyed: and the kingdom shall not be left to other people, but it shall break in pieces and consume all these kingdoms, and it shall stand for ever (Daniel 2:44).

There will be no united nation of Europe. Soon the kingdom of our Lord Jesus Christ will be established at His second coming. At that time, He will take the redeemed with Him to heaven. We can have great certainty concerning the definite failure for moves toward political union in Europe. No prophecy has ever failed to accurately reveal the future as clearly as if it was the past because every word of God is sure. Christ's second coming alone is our only hope for future unity.

This page intentionally left blank.

12

Blasphemous Claims

Some have wrongly identified the antichrist power as either an atheistic power, such as communism, or a pagan power, such as Hinduism or Buddhism. But this does not agree with the Scriptures. Paul testified that the antichrist power would possess the veneer of Christianity. It would be a power that actually claimed to be approved of God.

> He as God sitteth in the temple of God, shewing himself that he is God (2 Thessalonians 2:4).

Daniel also saw this power attempting to usurp the authority of Jesus.

> Yea, he magnified himself even to the prince of the host (Daniel 8:11).

John revealed that this false religious power would demand worship.

> And all that dwell upon the earth shall worship him, whose names are not written in the book of life

of the Lamb slain from the foundation of the world (Revelation 13:8).

He further declared that those who would not willingly worship the antichrist power would face death. Scripture indicates that an attempt will be made to enforce the worship of the antichrist throughout the entire world.

> And he had power to give life unto the image of the beast, that the image of the beast should both speak, and cause that as many as would not worship the image of the beast should be killed (Revelation 13:15).

This power is also described as a blasphemous power.

> And he shall speak great words against the most High, and shall wear out the saints of the most High, and think to change times and laws (Daniel 7:25).

> Who opposeth and exalteth himself above all that is called God, or that is worshipped; so that he as God sitteth in the temple of God, shewing himself that he is God (2 Thessalonians 2:4).

From the accusations made against Christ by the leaders of the Jews, we know the scriptural meaning of blasphemy. It means one who usurps the place of God.

> But Jesus held his peace. And the high priest answered and said unto him, I adjure thee by the living God, that thou tell us whether thou be the Christ, the Son of God. Jesus saith unto him, Thou hast said: nevertheless I say unto you , Hereafter shall ye see the Son of man sitting on the right hand of power, and coming in the clouds of heaven. Then the high priest rent his clothes, saying, He hath spoken blasphemy; what further need have we of witnesses? behold, now ye have heard his blasphemy (Matthew 26:63-65).

> And the high priest stood up in the midst, and asked Jesus, saying, Answerest thou nothing? what is it which these witness against thee? But he held his peace, and answered nothing. Again the high priest asked him, and said unto him, Art thou the Christ, the Son of the Blessed? And Jesus said, I am: and ye shall see the Son of man sitting on the right hand of power, and coming in the clouds of heaven. Then the high priest rent his clothes, and saith, What need we any further witnesses? Ye have heard the blasphemy: what think ye? And they all condemned him to be guilty of death (Mark 14:60-64).

The antichrist is appropriately designated by the name of blasphemy in Scripture.

> And I stood upon the sand of the sea, and saw a beast rise up out of the sea, having seven heads and ten horns, and upon his horns ten crowns, and upon his heads the name of blasphemy (Revelation 13:1).

This name indicates that the antichrist claims to be God or the Son of God. There is ample evidence that the papal church has frequently repeated such claims. Some striking examples are here cited:

> The priest may, in a certain manner, be called the creator of his Creator, since by saying the words of consecration, he creates, as it were, Jesus in the sacrament [the Eucharist] by giving him a sacramental existence. Oh happy function of the priest! He that created me (if I may say so) gave me power to create Him; and He that created me without me is Himself created by me (*Dignities and Duties of the Priest*, pp. 32, 33).

> Were the Redeemer to descend into a church, and sit in a confessional to administer the sacraments of penance, and a priest to sit in another confessional,

Jesus would say over each penitent, "Ego te absolvo" [I absolve you]. The priest would likewise say over each of his penitents, "Ego te absolvo," and the penitence of both would be equally absolved (*ibid.*, p. 28).

To pardon a single sin requires all the omnipotence of God. . . . But what only God can do by His omnipotence, the priest can also do by saying "Ego te absolvo. . . ." Indeed, it is not too much to say that, in view of the sublimity of their offices, the priests are so many gods (*ibid.*, pp. 34-36).

He [the priest] can hardly wait to each dawn when he will once again hold the Lord between his fingers [the wafer of the Mass]. . . . Our priests pick up the Lord and move Him here and there, forward and backward (*Our Sunday Visitor*, Dec. 1, 1946).

In December 1985, Russell and his wife, Enid, were present at a papal audience at the Vatican. At its conclusion, it was announced that the sins of all in attendance were absolved because of their presence there; and, further, Pope John Paul II had provided absolution for all of their loved ones! In a very real sense, the pope usurped a power above God, for he "forgave" the sins of men and women who offered no evidence of repentance.

Is it any wonder that the Scriptures describe the antichrist in such graphic terms?

Who opposeth and exalteth himself above all that is called God, or that is worshipped; so that he as God sitteth in the temple of God, shewing himself that he is God (2 Thessalonians 2:4).

And there was given unto him a mouth speaking great things and blasphemies (Revelation 13:5).

> And he opened his mouth in blasphemy against God, to blaspheme his name, and his tabernacle, and them that dwell in heaven (Revelation 13:6).

With such blasphemous claims, it is plain that the papacy cannot lead men and women to the kingdom of heaven. Obviously, such a power offers an invalid plan of redemption that will lead all its followers to eternal annihilation. Without doubt, the plan is a masterpiece of Satan. With the exception of God's saints, all the world will come under the hypnotic influence of the papacy.

In *Life* magazine of December 1989, Stefan Kanfer, in his incisive article, "The Triumph of John Paul II," dramatized the power of John Paul II. Kanfer details the pope's, step by victorious step, inside role in the extinction of the Communist Party in Poland. The prestige of the papacy had been put in a difficult position by the liberation theology of the Latin American Catholics. Kanfer pointed out that the communist collapse came at a most important time for the papacy because of the decline in church attendance in Western Europe and the liberal theology positions that were taken by many Catholics, both lay members and clergy in the United States.

Kanfer made a most significant observation when he said that the pope's "objective is not a holy war against communism, it is nothing less than the liberation of the world itself." He concluded his article with the perception that "the man who is likely to be remembered in the church's third millennium stands on the balcony of Saint Peter's Square, smiling down in delight and triumph, but not in surprise." Bible understanding Christians should not be surprised because the direction of these events is well-detailed in Holy Scripture.

It will again be seen that, just as soon as the Roman-Catholic-backed governments rise to power, oppression rather than freedom will result. Poland is already a striking example. The surprising rapidity of the movement toward total Catholic control in Poland can already be seen from reports concerning certain Protestant churches which were forbidden to distribute literature in that country. Solidarity has definitely made it clear that it will only recognize one church—the Roman Catholic Church.

Perhaps the most striking prophecy of Scripture points to the fact that, under the garb of peace, the papacy will yet destroy many.

> And through his policy also he shall cause craft to prosper in his hand; and he shall magnify himself in his heart, and *by peace shall destroy many*: he shall also stand up against the Prince of princes; but he shall be broken without hand (Daniel 8:25, emphasis added).

It is not surprising that "peace" is the greatest theme of contemporary Catholicism.

The accommodation of Catholicism, in its desire to bring all peoples under the umbrella of its authority, was no better demonstrated than during the World Day of Prayer for Peace on October 1986. On that day, Pope John Paul II met with many of the world religious leaders (Christian, pagan, even African witch doctors, and Togo snake handlers) at Assisi, Italy. All such meetings appear to be overtly under the canopy of Catholicism or as a prominent participant with the Catholic Church. The town of Assisi (made famous by Francis of Assisi, the Roman Catholic lover of nature and advocate of peace) has become a focal point for international prayer for peace. In 1989, a lot was said about Archbishop Runcie's pilgrimage to Assisi to pray for peace.

Jointly sponsored by the Costa Rican government and the Roman Catholic Church of Costa Rica, seven hundred international delegates met in San Jose on June 25-30, 1989, in order to discuss *peace* and *the new order* that it is hoped will be established in the twenty-first century. Here, marrying the pagan humanistic concepts of the New Age with Roman Catholic leadership, the chancellor of the United Nation's Peace University, Robert Muller, gave the keynote address.

> We must also hope that the pope will come before the year 2000 to the United Nations; speak for all the religions and spiritualities on this planet; and give the world the religious view of how the third millennium should be a spiritual millennium, a millennium which will see the integration and harmony of humanity (Muller's report in *Flashpoint*, January 1990).

The pope is the only public figure that has been suggested as the one who will oversee this world union. This is surely a most dramatic turn of events in human history.

On November 22, 1989, it was stated over the radio station, WJOY, that "the people of Eastern Europe are focusing their attention on Pope John Paul II for spiritual leadership in order to help bring about a peaceful solution to their political turmoil." Various religious leaders are urging their members to lay aside their differences, and work in unity under the banner of Rome. Some are even advocating church unification. The only response from Pope John Paul II was that "the issues separating our beliefs are not insurmountable; however, when it comes to ordination of women, birth control, and the Eucharist, Protestants must realize our assiduous position on these issues."

It is essential to recognize that this "unity" will always be on the basis of Protestant capitulation to Catholicism.

The pope's planned meeting of the approximate 1,000 European bishops, in 1991, was said to be for the purpose of "finding ways to meet the pope's vision of a Europe united in its Christian roots—including Eastern Europe after the fall of communism" (*U.S.A. Today,* April 23, 1990).

There is no question that the pope's goal is the unification of the whole world under his banner. The Christianity that the pope envisages is not biblical Christianity; instead, it is Roman Catholicism. A unity built on Roman Catholicism will lead to severe persecution of those who will not surrender to the leadership of the papacy.

> The weight of this world without God cannot be escaped by recourse to drugs, the misuse of sex, the culture of violence, or *joining sects*. This world must be conquered (Washington *Post*, April 23, 1989, emphasis added).

While we agree that God alone has the answer to mankind's needs, we fear the pope's statement that places the *joining of sects* with the evils of drugs, promiscuous sex, and violence. This statement indicates repressive actions against minority religions.

Bishop John Mooreman, the leader of the Anglican delegation of observers to the Second Vatican Council, was quoted as saying, "I think we realize that, if there is to be a final unity among Christians, there will have to be a central head of the church; and that head will clearly have to be the bishop of Rome."

Further, Bishop Oxman asserted, "I believe that union can and must be established in Christ's churches in the world. Since the Roman Catholic Church refuses . . . to accept union except on the basis of all other churches repudiating their own churches and returning to Rome, the first step toward union must be taken by the Protestant churches."

The ecumenical movement has sought to bind the churches together by a common Bible, established upon corrupt Greek texts. Almost all modern Bible translations are heavily dependent upon the Codex Sinaiticus and the Codex Vaticanus, two ancient Greek manuscripts from the Western Roman Empire, for the translation of the New Testament. Both have suffered from interpolations and deletions. So much is missing from the Vaticanus that it has sometimes been referred to as the abridged New Testament; thus hundreds of texts, or parts of texts, which are found in the European Bibles of the Reformation are not found in these modern translations. Nations as diverse as Italy, the Netherlands, and Hungary all have new ecumenical Bibles that are accepted by both Protestants and Catholics.

One of the great issues of the sixteenth and seventeenth centuries was Protestantism's unwavering support of the Greek manuscripts from the Eastern Roman Empire which were preserved with far greater integrity than those in the West. Today, these texts are commonly referred to as the

Textus Receptus (the Received Text or the Majority Text). A list of ecumenical hymns, which are thought suitable for singing in all churches, has also been established. All these are telltale signs of the false unity about to come.

There is every evidence that the blasphemous claims that are made by the papacy will be accepted by the majority of earth's inhabitants in the very near future.

13

False Principles of Salvation

A t first glance, the Catholic faith appears to be a complete gospel. John Wesley, the founder of Methodism, demonstrated that the gospel of the cross of Jesus embraced not only the justification, that was so beautifully presented by the sixteenth-century Reformers, but also sanctification. The gospel of Jesus is a complete gospel, encompassing justification (pardon and forgiveness) and sanctification (holiness, cleansing, and purification). The Bible is rich in verses that emphasize this understanding. We are justified by faith, and that same faith also sanctifies us.

> To open their eyes, and to turn them from darkness to light, and from the power of Satan unto God, that they may receive forgiveness of sins, and inheritance among them which are *sanctified by faith* that is in me (Acts 26:18, emphasis added).

The same sacrifice of Jesus that justifies also sanctifies.

> Husbands, love your wives, even as Christ also loved the church, and gave himself for it; that he might sanctify and cleanse it with the washing of water by the word, that he might present it to himself a glorious church, not having spot, or wrinkle, or any such thing; but that it should be holy and without blemish (Ephesians 5:25-27).
>
> Wherefore Jesus also, that he might sanctify the people with his own blood, suffered without the gate (Hebrews 13:12).
>
> By the which will we are sanctified through the offering of the body of Jesus Christ once for all (Hebrews 10:10).

The Council of Trent (1545-1563) was convened by the Roman Catholic Church in a desperate effort to counter the Protestant Reformation. Over the 18-year period of the council, the bishops discussed many issues, but few more vigorously than the issue of whether the gospel consisted of justification alone. This principle had been presented by the sixteenth-century Reformers. Eventually, by majority vote, the bishops upheld the concept that the gospel consisted of both justification and sanctification.

Some have subsequently claimed that those who believe that the gospel embraces sanctification along with justification are rejecting the Protestant Reformation and embracing a Catholic concept of the gospel. No conclusion could be further from the truth. It is essential to recognize that what was voted by the Council of Trent was not a true concept of either justification or sanctification. True justification and forgiveness takes place only in those who invite Christ to take control of their wills. He alone can transform the life, and turn us from wickedness unto holiness. Without that power, we are impotent to truly live the life of a Christian.

The sanctification that was espoused by the Council of Trent and the Roman Catholic Church is not based upon faith in Jesus; instead, it is works-oriented sacramentalism. Like the Jews of Christ's day who put their trust in ceremonialism (the doing of the sacrificial services and ordinances), the bishops of Rome voted that the keeping of the seven sacred sacraments (Mass, holy orders, marriage, baptism, penance, confirmation, and extreme unction) were meritorious for salvation. The statement of the bishops was the ultimate statement of a works gospel, a sanctification that is built upon sacramentalism.

This was exactly the legalism of the Jews that was condemned by Christ. It is a belief that works can merit salvation.

> Woe unto you, scribes and Pharisees, hypocrites! for ye pay tithe of mint and anise and cumin, and have omitted the weightier matters of the law, judgment, mercy, and faith: these ought ye to have done, and not to leave the other undone (Matthew 23:23).

> Many will say to me in that day, Lord, Lord, have we not prophesied in thy name? and in thy name have cast out devils? and in thy name done many wonderful works? And then will I profess unto them, I never knew you: depart from me, ye that work iniquity (Matthew 7:22, 23).

Authentic Christianity, while disavowing any hint of legalistic salvation, nevertheless accepts, by faith, Christ's merit and death to empower each one to live the life of victory. The sanctification that is understood by faithful Chris-

tians does not contain one whit of legalism or merit of
human works. It is established upon a sanctification that is
a gift of God through the merits of the sacrifice of Jesus
Christ;   thus genuine Christians constantly accept the
clearest testimony of Scripture that links justification and
sanctification together in the gospel. In so doing, they deny
the ceremonialism of the Jews and the sacramentalism of
the Roman Catholic Church. An example of works-oriented
concepts in the salvation of the Catholics can be seen in the
following statement:

> Faith alone will not save man, but good morals, or
> good works, are necessary (*The Convert's Catechism of
> Catholic Doctrine*, Tan Books and Publishers, Inc.,
> 1977).

The concept that salvation is merited by faith plus
human works is a pillar of the Roman Catholic apostasy.
While it is fully understood that no one can be saved
without good works because these are the inevitable
fruitage of sanctification, it must be adamantly stated that
there is no basis or merit in good works unto salvation.
Our salvation is only the result of the infinite grace of God,
through the merits of His Son, Jesus Christ;   thus personal
holiness is, in no measure, a basis of our salvation, but God
has declared it to be a condition upon which He bestows
His full salvation. As shown in the parable of the pearl of
great price, salvation is a free gift that costs our all. Only a
true Christian can comprehend this paradox.

It must be acknowledged that many Protestants have
been imprisoned by legalism, but the Word of God is explicit that the righteous live a life of faith. Some have so
strongly preached the law that they have almost ignored

the One who alone gives power to keep the law. God presents the law and faith together, and both are to be given equal weight because we cannot keep the commandments of God unless we have the faith of Jesus.

> Here is the patience of the saints: here are they that keep the commandments of God, and the faith of Jesus (Revelation 14:12).

The gospel of Jesus does not allow the barrenness of legalism or the powerlessness of antinomianism (the false doctrine that the observance of the law of God is irrelevant to salvation). The law and the gospel are inseparable "Siamese twins." To ignore one is to destroy them both.

The emphasis upon works, in the Roman Catholic Church, arises from the influence of paganism. The pagans, with their good gods and bad gods, focused upon ingratiating themselves to the good gods in a self-centered attempt to obtain all their benefits. They further attempted to appease the bad gods in order to avoid receiving their curses; thus pagans build their worship upon a ceaseless round of activities, ceremonies, and sacraments in a futile effort to achieve their goal. In many Buddhist temples, both good gods and devil gods are worshiped. In the famous Burmah Road Buddhist Temple, in Penang, Malaysia, there are, in addition to good gods, two gods with opium streaming from their mouths. These idols, which are designated as devil gods, are earnestly entreated by their worshipers.

As the early Christian church more and more imbibed the pagan philosophy of the former Roman Empire and embraced its principles, it began to institute rounds of works-oriented practices which were taught to be essential to human salvation. The unconverted have always preferred such works-oriented practices over a dependent faith in Jesus. Such a belief appeals to the checklist mentality which lulls us into carnal security. A simple compliance with the minimum requirements for salvation will not save even one soul. Such does not require a transformation of heart. The natural human heart may meet all the checklist items as did the rich young ruler. It may feel secure in conforming to all these requirements; however, the individual may be moving headlong toward eternal oblivion while his priest assures him that he has secured eternal life.

The medieval Roman Catholic Church had developed this works-based brand of salvation into a refined art. Through confession to the priest, penance, the payment of monies, pilgrimages, attendance at ritual services, and other acts, the individual was made to feel a deep sense of security when his heart was still carnal. The Jews of Christ's day had, in the same way, learned to depend upon human effort for salvation. They had based their hope of salvation upon fulfilling the most detailed obligations of both the Torah (God's Word) and the Mishnah (man's word). Both the Jews and the Roman Catholics have forgotten the divine principles of salvation in their consideration of the acts of obedience to merit their salvation.

> Behold, thou desirest truth in the inward parts: and in the hidden part thou shalt make me to know wisdom. Purge me with hyssop, and I shall be clean: wash me, and I shall be whiter than snow. Create in me a clean heart, O God; and renew a right spirit

within me. Restore unto me the joy of thy salvation; and uphold me with thy free spirit. Then will I teach transgressors thy ways; and sinners shall be converted unto thee. For thou desirest not sacrifice; else would I give it: thou delightest not in burnt offering. The sacrifices of God are a broken spirit: a broken and a contrite heart, O God, thou wilt not despise (Psalm 51:6, 7, 10, 12, 13, 16, 17).

The great message of righteousness by faith in Jesus must be proclaimed at the end of the world. Satan has used the Roman Catholic concept of sanctification to discredit the truth of true sanctification by faith. Colin well-remembers that a prominent Protestant theologian, in a dialogue, said, "Sanctification is a good principle, but it is not part of the gospel."

The Bible is rich with statements that link justification with sanctification in the gospel. But before sharing these with the reader, let us once more make clear what these terms really mean. Justification is simply divine forgiveness and pardon, which restores individuals to a position before God as if they had never sinned. Sanctification refers to the cleansing and purification of the soul. In the New Testament, justification is synonymous with the term, *righteousness;* and sanctification is synonymous with the term, *holiness.*

When we confess our sins (which crucified our Saviour) with deep repentance, we are forgiven and justified. In the sight of God, our sins are no more. We stand righteous before God as we accept, through faith, the perfect merits and grace of the One who has had victory over sin and died for us.

> Even when we were dead in sins, hath quickened
> us together with Christ, (by grace ye are saved;) For
> by grace are ye saved through faith; and that not of
> yourselves: it is the gift of God: not of works, lest any
> man should boast (Ephesians 2:5, 8, 9).

God is so good. He not only provides, through Christ,
the divine power to forgive but also restores. It is not His
purpose that we should continue to live a life of sin which
engenders guilt, condemnation, and low self-esteem. He
desires to keep His people from falling back into sin. His
love provides the forgiveness of our sins, through Christ.
He also provides the power to keep His faithful children
from returning to their sin. Now, it has to be acknowledged
that many faithful Christians have fallen back into sin. The
moment we take our eyes off Jesus, we certainly become
vulnerable to the assaults of Satan. The wonderful thing is
that we are not rejected because we failed our Lord.

> My little children, these things write I unto you,
> that ye sin not. And if any man sin, we have an advo-
> cate with the Father, Jesus Christ the righteous (1 John
> 2:1).

It is in God's plan for His children that they should, relying upon His power moment by moment, live a life free
from the bondage of sin.

Let us examine a selection of the many texts that unite
justification and sanctification as inseparable aspects of our
salvation.

> If we confess our sins, he is faithful and just to for-
> give us our sins [justification], and to cleanse us from
> all unrighteousness [sanctification] (1 John 1:9).

> There is therefore now no condemnation to them
> which are in Christ Jesus [justification], who walk not

after the flesh, but after the Spirit [sanctification] (Romans 8:1).

To open their eyes, and to turn them from darkness to light, and from the power of Satan unto God, that they may receive forgiveness of sins [justification], and inheritance among them which are sanctified by faith that is in me (Acts 26:18).

Jesus answered, Verily, verily, I say unto thee, Except a man be born of water [justification] and of the Spirit [sanctification], he cannot enter into the kingdom of God (John 3:5).

For he hath made him to be sin for us, who knew no sin [justification]; that we might be made the righteousness of God in him [sanctification] (2 Corinthians 5:21).

It is most important that those whom God will redeem are both justified and sanctified.

He that is unjust, let him be unjust still: and he which is filthy, let him be filthy still: and he that is righteous [justified], let him be righteous still: and he that is holy [sanctified], let him be holy still (Revelation 22:11).

There are Protestants who have stated that the linking of sanctification together with justification in the gospel is spiritual adultery. They believe this because they have accepted the works concept of sanctification that is espoused by the Roman Catholic Church instead of the biblical concept of sanctification by faith; thus they have concluded that it is unthinkable to ascribe any merit for salvation to human effort. In this, they are correct because there cannot be one shred of merit in human effort, even that motivated by the Holy Spirit. Important as the strongest efforts of the human will are, they are no basis whatsoever for our salvation. Our salvation is assured, as we have said earlier, on the basis of Christ's grace alone; thus the Bible teaches that we are both justified and sanctified by God through the life, death, and high priestly ministry of the Son of God. When this is properly understood, we need not fear the works-oriented sanctification that is espoused by the Roman Catholic Church. It is a crude counterfeit of true sanctification.

In the loving power of the Saviour, God will have a people who truly reflect His character.

> And to her [God's church] was granted that she should be arrayed in fine linen, clean and white: for the fine linen is the righteousness of saints (Revelation 19:8).

> And I looked, and, lo, a Lamb stood on the mount Sion, and with him an hundred forty and four thousand, having his Father's name written in their foreheads. These are they which were not defiled with women; for they are virgins. These are they which follow the Lamb whithersoever he goeth. These were redeemed from among men, being the firstfruits unto God and to the Lamb. And in their mouth was found no guile: for they are without fault before the throne of God (Revelation 14:1, 4, 5).

> Husbands, love your wives, even as Christ also loved the church, and gave himself for it; that he might sanctify and cleanse it with the washing of water by the word, that he might present it to himself a glorious church, not having spot, or wrinkle, or any such thing; but that it should be holy and without blemish (Ephesians 5:25-27).

Now unto him that is able to keep you from falling, and to present you faultless before the presence of his glory with exceeding joy (Jude 24).

The remnant of Israel shall not do iniquity, nor speak lies; neither shall a deceitful tongue be found in their mouth: for they shall feed and lie down, and none shall make them afraid (Zephaniah 3:13).

For the grace of God that bringeth salvation hath appeared to all men, teaching us that, denying ungodliness and worldly lusts, we should live soberly, righteously, and godly, in this present world; looking for that blessed hope, and the glorious appearing of the great God and our Saviour Jesus Christ; who gave himself for us, that he might redeem us from all iniquity, and purify unto himself a peculiar people, zealous of good works (Titus 2:11-14).

Sadly, neither the Roman Catholic Church nor many of the Protestant churches teach the biblical principle of salvation through faith; as a consequence, they are denying their members the knowledge of the principles by which only God's people will be prepared for Christ's return. It takes a day-by-day commitment of our lives to Jesus, allowing Him to work in us to make such a preparation.

Work out your own salvation with fear and trembling. For it is God which worketh in you both to will and to do of his good pleasure (Philippians 2:12, 13).

This page intentionally left blank.

14

The Deadly Wound Re-examined

Serious students of Bible prophecy have been fascinated for a long time with the deadly wound of the beast of Revelation 13 and its healing.

> And I saw one of his heads as it were wounded to death; and his deadly wound was healed: and all the world wondered after the beast (Revelation 13:3).

We have seen that the deadly wound was inflicted upon the papacy in 1798, when General Berthier, of Napoleon's army, took the pope a captive to France. This wound was further deepened in 1870, when Giuseppe Garibaldi seized all the territory of the Papal States and incorporated it into the new kingdom of Italy; thus the papacy had been stripped of its last vestige of temporal power, a power it had exerted since A.D. 538.

In reality, Rome fell to Italian forces that were led by General Raffaele Cadorna on September 20, 1870. Pope Pius IX capitulated, and a national vote was taken in the

Papal States, in October 1870, which resulted in an overwhelming majority in favor of union with Italy. The event
which stimulated the overthrow of the Papal States is significant to the student of God's Word.

> The way had been paved by the meeting of the
> [first] Vatican Council, in 1869-1870, and its proclama-
> tion, in July 1870, of the infallibility of the pope. This
> symptom of the increasing centralization and
> clericalization of the church revived some of the old
> opposition (*Encyclopedia Britannica*, 1963 edition, sub-
> ject: Italy).

The relationship of the declaration of the unscriptural
doctrine of papal infallibility and the resultant loss of
Vatican sovereignty over the Papal States is frequently
overlooked. The papacy had caused its own downfall.

The healing process was initiated by Benito Mussolini,
prime minister of Italy, who, in 1929, signed the Lateran
Treaty which restored temporal power to the papacy by
returning its possession of the territory of Vatican City.
This territory, just a mere speck of Rome that occupies only
108 acres (one sixth of a square mile), has become the center of the most powerful political organization upon earth.
As succeeding popes have strengthened their influence
upon the destinies of nations, the wound has healed so effectively that it is now almost impossible to detect even the
scar.

When Pope Pius XII died in 1958, it appeared that the
College of Cardinals could not decide on a suitable replace-
ment. As a temporary measure, they chose the elderly Cardinal Roncalli as Pius XII's successor. In four and a half
years, as Pope John XXIII, he completely changed the face

of Catholicism, and dispelled the antagonism of most Protestants.

Upon the death of John XXIII in 1963, the archbishop of Milan, Cardinal Montini, was elected Pope Paul VI. In the fifteen years of his pontificate, Paul VI introduced a schedule of worldwide travel for himself that had never before been undertaken by a pope. In this manner, he became an international figure. While he did not possess the charisma of John XXIII, he nevertheless rode on a wave of Catholic popularity that was generated by his predecessor.

With the death of Paul VI in 1978, Cardinal Luciani, archbishop of Venice, was voted to fill the papal seat. He assumed the title of John Paul I. His sudden death, after a mere 33 days in office, precipitated a return of the cardinals to the Sistine Chapel, in the Vatican, in order to elect another man to the papal throne. For over 400 years, the choice of a pope had always been an Italian. It was not anticipated, on this occasion, that there would be any deviation from this precedence.

All evidence, at the time, indicated that this was indeed a fierce, close contest in the early ballots between the archbishop of Milan and the archbishop of Naples. But neither could obtain the two-thirds majority vote that is required for papal election; thus the College of Cardinals turned its attention to a compromise candidate. To the amazement of the world, a Polish prelate (Cardinal Karol Wojtyla, archbishop of Cracow) was appointed. He was not even the primate of Poland (that appointment, at the time, was held by the archbishop of Warsaw); yet this unlikely selection has proven to be an act of pure genius in the fulfillment of the aims and political ambitions of the Roman Catholic Church. No pope has ever prepared the way for a greater fulfillment of Bible prophecy than has this former armaments factory worker from Poland.

Today, Pope John Paul II has gained the respect and applause of almost all peoples of every nation. He is seen as a peacemaker, a champion of underprivileged nations, and an upholder of democracy. Such a reputation is amazing for the head of a power which has the worst record of any in the field of democracy. This power has a record of belligerence second to none, and has kept more nations in a state of poverty and backwardness than any other power in the history of this world.

The noted Catholic scholar, Peter de Rosa (former professor of metaphysics and ethics at Westminster Seminary; dean of Corpus Christi College, in London; and a former Jesuit priest who was trained in the Gregorian University in Rome), had this to say concerning the Roman Catholic record of justice:

> The record of the Inquisition would be embarrassing for any organization; for the Catholic Church, it is devastating. Today, it prides itself, and with much justification [the authors would dispute this judgment], on being the defender of natural law and the rights of man. The papacy, in particular, likes to see itself as the champion of morality. What history shows is that, for more than six centuries without a break, the papacy was the sworn enemy of elementary justice. Of eighty popes in a line from the thirteenth century on, not one of them disapproved of the theology and apparatus of Inquisition. On the contrary, one after another added his own cruel touches to the

> workings of the deadly machine (Peter de Rosa, *Vicars of Christ*, Corgi Books, 1989, p. 244).

The Bible had declared that, notwithstanding this truly abysmal track record, all the world would regard the papacy with wonderment.

We have seen evidence of this even among the Protestant churches which were originally established to throw off the unmatched evils and errors of the Roman Catholic Church. Many Anglicans, Lutherans, Baptists, and others now see no peril in establishing close relationships with the Roman Catholic Church. In this, they are utterly blind. Even Billy Graham has proclaimed Pope John Paul II as the most significant religious figure in the present world.

> It is not without reason that the claim has been put forth in Protestant countries that Catholicism differs less widely from Protestantism than in former times. There has been a change; but the change is not in the papacy. Catholicism indeed resembles much of the Protestantism that now exists, because Protestantism has so greatly degenerated since the days of the Reformers (Ellen White. *The Great Controversy*, p. 571).

The calls of the archbishop of Canterbury to elevate the pope to spiritual leader of Christendom falls upon deaf ears when suggested to those who believe Bible prophecy. Such men and women are appalled by the lack of spiritual insight shown by churches such as the Lutheran and Southern Baptist churches. Still there are numerous men and women who doubt the ability of the Roman Catholic Church to hold sway over the atheistic and non-Christian world.

Recent events in communist Europe have shown the error of such complacency. Once it was believed that communism and Catholicism were irreconcilable enemies.

> The meeting of the pope and Mr. Gorbachev, in December 1989, indicated to the world the symbolic end of the twentieth century's most dramatic spiritual war, a conflict in which the seemingly irresistible force of communism battered against the immovable object of Christianity (*Time* magazine, Australian Edition, December 4, 1989).

Time has revealed the truth of Bible prophecy which indicates that *all* the world will wonder after the beast. Mr. Gorbachev's visit to the Vatican, in December 1989, was an immensely significant act. Prior to that visit, he had taken the unprecedented step to seek the pope's assistance in order to help him calm the Catholic citizens in the Ukraine.

Stalin thought that the Vatican was weak. At the Postsdam Conference, in 1945, Stalin had scornfully asked Churchill, "How many divisions did you say the pope had?" Gorbachev found that the pope has many *divisions* of loyal followers on the streets of the cities of the Ukraine and Lithuania.

Gorbachev well-knew that the pope could not be trusted to quiet the voice of revolt in areas of Catholic concentrations unless he offered to fulfill the Vatican's objectives; thus, in anticipating his meeting with John Paul II, it was stated that he would offer the following inducements:

> "Come to Moscow and other Soviet cities on an official tour," he [Gorbachev] will say. "Talk of peaceful change to your co-religionists in the Ukraine and in separatist Lithuania as well; urge them, as Cardinal Glemp did in Poland years ago, to be patient and not

to seek to overthrow the political regime" (Singapore *Straits Times*, Nov. 13, 1989).

Gorbachev offered to undo "Stalin's forced amalgamation and subjugation" (*ibid.*) of the Roman Catholic Church with the Russian Orthodox Church; furthermore, the Soviet leader planned to return the seized church properties, and to permit the reopening of Roman Catholic schools in the U.S.S.R.

The author of the article cited above, William Safire of the New *York Times*, perceptively referred to this.

> The pope will want to use the opportunity offered by Mr. Gorbachev as a lever to help end the schism in the church. With that theological motive, he is likely to strike a political deal (*ibid.*).

The schism here that is referred to is between the Russian Orthodox and Roman Catholic churches.

Gorbachev, notwithstanding some progressive moves in Eastern Europe, demonstrated absolutely no insight in opening up his country to the inroads of Roman Catholicism in this way. Religious freedom is one thing; facilitating Roman Catholic expansionist ambitions is entirely another. But here before our eyes is clear evidence of the escalating favor that's afforded to the Roman Catholic Church by communist regimes—*all* the world wondered after the beast.

In spite of all the efforts during 40 years of communist rule, Catholicism may be stronger today in Eastern Europe than before communism.

> After 40 years of suppression, Christian democracy is finding its natural constituency in tact across Central Europe. In Slovakia, the Hungarian provinces,

and rural Poland electorates are overwhelmingly Catholic, conservative, and cautious. Despite the iniquities of the postwar years, the church has maintained massive influence, all the more now that it has been a focus of moral resistance to communism. . . . Here lies the obvious danger inherent in the rightwing revival: A church sponsored eruption of nationalism and obscurantism that already threatens the stable development of democracy in Eastern Europe (Singapore *Straits Times,* April 17, 1990).

It was not surprising that Hungary, formerly one of the staunchest opponents of Catholicism, resumed diplomatic relations with the Vatican on February 9, 1990 (*Newsweek,* Feb. 19, 1990). It was Hungary which had, in 1948, imprisoned Cardinal Mindszenty, Roman Catholic primate of Hungary. During the 1956 uprising, the cardinal fled to the American Embassy in Budapest where he spent almost two decades in political asylum before dying in exile in Austria during 1975. But now Hungary is "wondering after the beast" in fulfillment of the prophetic Word. Poland had, in July 1989, been the first Eastern bloc country to open diplomatic relations with the Vatican. The U.S.S.R. and the Vatican resumed diplomatic relations on March 15, 1990.

In March 1990, two significant events occurred in Romania. Though Romania has less than three million Roman Catholics and Eastern Rite Catholics among its twenty-three million inhabitants, its importance in the papal schemes of the future has not escaped the attention of the pope. The return of the Vatican Embassy that was confiscated by the communist leaders in Romania 40 years ago was the most significant. In the same month, John Paul II named 12 new bishops for Romania—seven Roman

Catholics and five Eastern Rite bishops. He also elevated two former underground bishops to the rank of archbishop. There was no resistance from the new leaders of Romania. Talk of a return to diplomatic relations with the Vatican was then heard. Romania established diplomatic relations with the Vatican on May 15, 1990.

The pope is also anxious to obtain the cooperation of the Orthodox churches of Europe.

> He visited [in 1979] the Orthodox patriarch of Constantinople, with an objective that was not obvious even to his Vatican associates. The patriarch is the spiritual head of all Orthodox churches in the world. Through him, Karol Wojtyla [Pope John Paul II] wanted to convey the same message to Eastern Europe's Orthodox churches: Communism's collapse is near, be ready to fill the vacuum (Enrico Jacchia, of the *International Herald Tribune*, in the Singapore *Straits Times*, March 13, 1990).

No wonder the pope sees that "a new European political order will be set up, and the goodwill of a cooperative Soviet leadership in shaping it is of utmost importance" (*ibid.*).

Not only are the Soviets supporting such a unity but the leadership of the United States is also.

> He [President Bush] said he was resolutely in favor of a united and peaceful Germany in a united and peaceful Europe (Singapore *Straits Times*, April 15, 1990).

The U.S.S.R.'s tacit permission of Roman Catholic Lithuania's succession from the U.S.S.R that was declared by the Lithuanian parliament on March 12, 1990, demonstrates how powerful the papal influence is upon

the Kremlin. Many may wonder why Lithuania, a country
of a mere 3.6 million people, would dare to challenge the
strong power of the U.S.S.R., the third most populous nation upon earth with 280 million people. Such do not understand that feverish activity by the Roman Catholic
hierarchy is undoubtedly supporting the Lithuanian
people. It must be recognized that Mr. Gorbachev dare not
antagonize the papacy lest such action incites the Catholics,
in the strategically important Ukraine, to revolution; thus,
in a very real sense, the president of the U.S.S.R. is greatly
limited in his opinions in dealing with this small territory.
Sending in the Red Army, which could easily settle the
issue of secession, is certainly not a likely option that is
presently open to the Russian leadership. Such an action
would alienate the Vatican and seriously threaten
Gorbachev's position. Incredibly, the world's smallest nation, a minuscule one sixth of a square mile, is effectively
dominating earth's largest nation that consists of over eight
and a half million square miles. Only an omniscient God
would have foreseen such an unlikely situation; thus the
communist world, for reasons of political expediency, at
present has little option except to "wonder after the beast."

We can expect to see much posturing by the U.S.S.R.
over Lithuania's unilateral declaration of independence.
This has already been seen with the occupation of the head-
quarters of the Lithuanian Communist Party, the rounding
up of Lithuanian deserters from the Red Army, the movement of tanks through the capital city, Vilnius, and similar
actions.

But, Gorbachev's saber rattling aside, there is every
indication he believes the three republics have the

right to secede, though only after Moscow has agreed to the terms of separation (*Time* magazine, April 2, 1990).

The Vatican's pressure has undoubtedly caused Gorbachev to come to such a conclusion. Lenin, Stalin, Malenkov, Kruschev, and other Soviet leaders would simply have marched a few battalions of the four million strong Red Army into Lithuania (total population only 3.6 million), and that would have speedily ended the matter. In 1956, the independence movement in Hungary, a nation far stronger than Lithuania, was quelled in a few days. Similarly, in 1968, Czechoslovak moves toward democracy were put down because of the Russian military machine. Due to the pope's intervention in Soviet affairs, the Soviet response to the declared independence of Lithuania is expected to be different.

Western observers concurred that a full-scale invasion [of Lithuania] was unlikely. "What we see now is Gorbachev raising the ante in what will be hard and drawn-out negotiations," said an American diplomat in Moscow. "Lithuania has a united population on the issue of independence, and I don't think they'll back down. And Moscow has pretty well ruled out force." At independence ceremonies in Namibia last week, Soviet Foreign Minister Eduard Shevardnadze said, "We are against the use of force in any region, and we are particularly against the use of force domestically" (*ibid.*).

Unquestionably, the pope is playing a decisive role in what is happening in Lithuania.

The pope, on Saturday [April 14], met Soviet President Mikhail Gorbachev's personal adviser, Vadim Zagladin, for talks believed to have touched on

Lithuania. He also issued a message of support to
Lithuanian Roman Catholic Church leaders, saying he
felt closer than ever to the aspirations of the
Lithuanian people! The Vatican's ambassador to Moscow, last week, indicated that the Vatican was willing
to act as a mediator in the Lithuanian crisis if both
sides wanted. Italian Communist Party newspaper,
Unita, said Mr. Zagladin had been sent by Mr. Gorbachev to examine how the Vatican could play a role
in ending the face-off between the Kremlin and the
Baltic Republic which declared itself independent on
March 11 (Singapore *Straits Times*, April 16, 1990).

On March 18, 1990, East Germany held its first
democratic elections. Incredibly, the Christian Democrat
Party, the party of the Roman Catholic Church, easily
emerged as the most successful of the 21 parties that con-
tested the polls. They received over 40 percent of the votes
while their closest rivals, the Social Democrats, received 24
percent, and the party for Social Democracy (the reformed
Communist Party) received 16 percent. The success of the
Christian Democrat Party was remarkable, not only because it was achieved in a nation that had been avowedly
communist for over 40 years but because East Germany includes German territories which were overwhelmingly
Lutheran prior to the advent of communism. The results of
this election certainly demonstrated the efficiency of the
Roman Catholic Church even in communist nations which
were former strongholds of Protestantism.

In the non-Christian world, there is no greater foe to
Catholicism than Islam; yet even, in this sphere,
Catholicism is making giant strides. When, in the 1930s,
the Islamic population in Rome requested permission from

Mussolini to build a mosque in Rome, he replied with an emphatic "No! When we can build a Roman Catholic church in Mecca, you can build a mosque in Rome." Mussolini's statement at least contained a marginal level of logic.

But today a $50,000,000 mosque is under construction in Rome with Vatican approval. The head of the mosque, Prince Abolghassem Amini, has openly stated his great admiration of Pope John Paul II. He has expressed a desire for closer Islamic links with the Vatican (*Sarawak Tribune*, Malaysia, March 8, 1989).

Is it any wonder that the Reuter's correspondent who reported this matter perceptively declared, in speaking about the construction of the mosque, "Its religious and political symbolism is very important, *a sign of the times*" (*ibid.*, emphasis added). It is indeed a sign of the times vastly more significant than the reporter recognized. The architect of the mosque, Vittorio Gigliotti, also insightfully exclaimed, "This is a work of exceptional historic, religious, cultural and political importance. It will have tremendous impact upon public opinion!" (*ibid.*).

When Pope John Paul II visited Indonesia in 1989, hordes of citizens of that nation flocked to his meetings, despite the fact that its population is predominately Islamic.

Similar crowds of unprecedented proportions attended the papal gatherings in Buddhist Singapore and Thailand, as well as Hindu India, on previous visits. Truly *all* the world is wondering after the beast. Pope John Paul II has been seen by more individuals than any other human in the entire history of the world. Bible prophecy is being fulfilled in our time with unerring accuracy. How alert we must be if we are to be prepared for the serious crisis ahead, when Roman Catholicism will once more seek to force its errors upon the consciences of true men and women by using the arm of political power. She will not disdain from the use of fearful persecution anymore than she did in the past.

When church leaders such as the archbishop of Canterbury openly recognize the papacy as the head of all the Christian churches, they are ignoring the potent lessons of history as expressed by President Roosevelt.

> Those who have long enjoyed such privileges as we enjoy forget in time that men have died to win them (*Life*, March, 1990).

15

Seven-Headed Monsters

Three seven-headed monsters are described in the book of Revelation.

1. And there appeared another wonder in heaven; and behold a great red dragon, having seven heads and ten horns, and seven crowns upon his heads (Revelation 12:3).

2. And I stood upon the sand of the sea, and saw a beast rise out of the sea, having seven heads and ten horns, and upon his horns ten crowns, and upon his heads the name of blasphemy. And the beast which I saw was like unto a leopard, and his feet were as the feet of a bear, and his mouth as the mouth of a lion: and the dragon gave him his power, and his seat, and great authority (Revelation 13:1, 2).

3. So he carried me away in the spirit into the wilderness: and I saw a woman sit upon a scarlet coloured beast, full of names of blasphemy, having seven heads and ten horns (Revelation 17:3).

Many Christians have found these symbolic beasts to be incomprehensible. But God intended the book of Revelation to be understood.

> Blessed is he that readeth, and they that hear the
> words of this prophecy (Revelation 1:3).

Fortunately, the Bible is its own expositor. Let us first examine the first seven-headed monster—the dragon beast. God does not leave us in the least doubt about who is represented by this beast.

> And the great dragon was cast out, that old serpent,
> called the Devil, and Satan, which deceiveth the whole
> world (Revelation 12:9).

Satan uses human instrumentalities to pursue his nefarious schemes. The following prophecy refers to God's church as a pure woman and Christ as her child.

> The dragon stood before the woman that was ready
> to be delivered, for to devour her child as soon as it
> was born (Revelation 12:4).

At the time of Christ's birth, King Herod, a vassal of the Roman Empire, was ruler in Judea. In order to destroy the baby Jesus, whom Herod feared as a potential rival, he had all males under 2 years old slaughtered.

> Then Herod, when he saw that he was mocked of
> the wise men, was exceeding wroth, and sent forth,
> and slew all the children that were in Bethlehem, and
> in all the coasts thereof (Matthew 2:16).

Christ's life was saved only because God intervened by warning Joseph to flee with Him to Egypt. But Satan had done his utmost, using the human arm of the Roman Empire, to destroy Christ before His ministry commenced; thus the seven-headed monster of Revelation 12 illustrates the fact that all counterfeit religions, which inevitably oppose God's truth, are motivated by Satan. In this sense, the dragon of Revelation 12 is a key to our understanding of all the beasts of prophecy.

Many have wondered why God uses beasts to symbolize nations; yet such individuals do not question the use of such symbolism in the secular world today. A few years ago, when there was a major border dispute between China and the U.S.S.R., *Asiaweek* magazine printed a cover illustration that depicted a fierce bear and an enraged panda fighting. Only a most ill-informed reader would have needed to be enlightened concerning which nations were represented here; likewise, countries represent their sporting teams in symbols of animals and birds. In Rugby League, the Australian team is called the Kangaroos and the New Zealand team, the Kiwis. In Rugby Union, the British team is referred to as the Lions; the South African team, the Springboks; and the Australian team, the Wallabies. Americans frequently use the eagle as the symbol of their nation. France uses the cockerel, and Thailand uses the elephant; thus God, in His wisdom, uses a form of symbolism that's well-understood by mankind.

The second seven-headed monster has a more specific meaning, although still motivated by the demonic power of Satan. Notice that this beast was a combination of the features of a leopard, a bear, and a lion. These characteristics undoubtedly refer to the symbolic animals of the great prophecy of Daniel 7. In that prophetic outline, the lion symbolized Babylon; the bear symbolized Medo-Persia; and the leopard symbolized Greece. This second seven-headed monster evidently possesses the evil characteristics of the enemies of God's truth and His people.

The second monster is identified by the description of its activities and the duration of its reign.

> And there was given unto him a mouth speaking great things and blasphemies; and power was given unto him to continue forty and two months. And he opened his mouth in blasphemy against God, to blaspheme his name, and his tabernacle, and them that dwell in heaven. And it was given unto him to make war with the saints, and to overcome them: and power was given him over all kindreds, and tongues, and nations (Revelation 13:5-7).

The period of papal dominance during the 1260 years is here reiterated. Each Jewish month consisted of 30 days; thus 42 months equals 1260 days. As previously shown, a prophetic day is symbolic of a literal year. Papal Rome dominated Europe and, later, much of the world for precisely 1260 years. Since the year A.D. 538 (when the Ostrogoths were driven out), the Roman emperor permitted the pope to implement Emperor Justinian's edict of A.D. 533. This made him the head of all the churches. Papal authority was maintained in Europe until the pope was made a prisoner by Napoleon in 1798.

Let us note the other identifying characteristics that are cited, including the persecution of God's people and blasphemy against God and His tabernacle. Daniel prophetically attributes these precise characteristics to the little-horn power which also represents the papacy.

> And he shall speak great words against the most High, and shall wear out the saints of the most High, and think to change times and laws: and they shall be given into his hand until a time and times and the dividing of time (Daniel 7:25).

Note that the blasphemy against God and the persecution of His saints function together during a specific period of time—"time and times and the dividing of time." These time periods literally refer to one year, two years, and half a year—a total of three and a half years. The Jewish year consists of 12 months each of 30 days; thus a Jewish year was 360 days in length. Simple multiplication of 360 by three and a half provides the figure of 1260 prophetic days or literal years, precisely identical to the time that's specified in Revelation 13.

All three monsters possess ten horns. The book of Daniel once more assists us in unfolding the mystery of these symbols, for the fourth beast of Daniel 7 also possessed ten horns. Daniel represented the Roman Empire by the symbolic fourth breast.

> And the ten horns out of this kingdom are ten kings
> that shall arise (Daniel 7:24).

Revelation 13:1 records that each of the ten horns possesses a crown. The Roman Empire fractured into the ten kingdoms of Western Europe—the Huns, Ostrogoths, Visigoths, Franks, Vandals, Suevi, Burgundians, Heruli, Lombards, and Anglo-Saxons. Today, these tribes largely constitute the European nations. The presence of the ten horns indicates both the location of the papacy in Europe and the powerful support given to it, by the nations of that continent, during the era of its supremacy.

The thirteenth chapter of Revelation, as we have seen, also depicts a lamb-like beast with two horns which gave power to this second monster after it had received the deadly wound (Revelation 13:11-17). We shall see more of this beast later.

The third seven-headed monster (of Revelation, chapter 17) is greatly significant to this present era. This beast also has ten horns, but they are uncrowned. And a whore sat upon the beast.

> And the woman was arrayed in purple and scarlet colour, and decked with gold and precious stones and pearls, having a golden cup in her hand full of abominations and filthiness of her fornication: and upon her forehead was a name written, MYSTERY, BABYLON THE GREAT, THE MOTHER OF HAR-LOTS AND ABOMINATIONS OF THE EARTH. And I saw the woman drunken with the blood of the saints, and with the blood of the martyrs of Jesus: and when I saw her, I wondered with great admiration (Revelation 17:4-6).

This woman of ill-fame represents the evil counterfeit religion of Babylon, in various guises, which has viciously oppressed God's people. The religion of modern Babylon was derived from the religion of ancient Babylon which also formed the basis of the religions of Medo-Persia, Greece, Pagan Rome, and Papal Rome. Although Babylon was utterly destroyed many centuries ago, her religion remains very much alive in all the apostate faiths that are based upon its false dogma.[1]

This woman can justifiably be seen riding upon each of the beasts which represent the great forces in opposition to God's pure truth. This red colored seven-headed monster is merely another aspect of the same satanic power. The iden-tification of this power will be discovered in the following chapter.

Endnote

[1] For a more complete discussion of this matter, see Adventism Proclaimed by the same authors. Write to Hartland Publications, P. O. Box 1, Rapidan, Virginia 22733, U.S.A.

This page intentionally blank.

16

The Mystery of the Seven Heads

The Bible gives us the clue that the unravels the mystery of the third seven-headed monster.

> And here is the mind which hath wisdom. The seven heads are seven mountains, on which the woman sitteth. And there are seven kings: five are fallen, and one is, and the other is not yet come; and when he cometh, he must continue a short space. And the beast that was, and is not, even he is the eighth, and is of the seven, and goeth into perdition (Revelation 17:9-11).

In Scripture, a mountain is symbolic of a nation or kingdom. In the following text, God is speaking about the Babylonian Empire:

> Behold, I am against thee, O destroying mountain, saith the Lord (Jeremiah 51:25).

It should not surprise us that the seven kings are associated with the seven mountains.

Exponents of prophecy have long pondered the mystery of the five fallen heads, the one present, and the one in the future. Various explanations have been suggested. Most of these explanations have assumed that the one that "is" is a power that is contemporaneous with the period in which the book of Revelation was written.

One of the greatest nineteenth-century exponents of the prophecies of Daniel and Revelation, Uriah Smith, suggested that the seven heads represented the seven types of government that were in control during the era of the Roman Empire—kingly, consular, decemviral, dictatorial, triumviral, imperialist, and papal (Uriah Smith. *Daniel and the Revelation*, Signs Publishing Company, p. 669).

We greatly admire Uriah Smith's work, but this explanation does not fit the criteria as we shall see. These heads evidently represent individual powers rather than various aspects of a single power.

The view that the head that "is" represents Pagan Rome (the power in ascendancy during the period in which John wrote the book of Revelation) remains popular. Using this basis for the sixth kingdom, these interpreters have suggested that the five fallen kingdoms were Egypt, Assyria, Babylon, Medo-Persia, and Greece. The seventh kingdom which is yet to come, by this understanding, was Papal Rome. But this interpretation may be faulted on two grounds. Firstly, Egypt and Assyria never appear in God's great list of world apostate powers that are represented in the books of Daniel and Revelation. Secondly, what the Bible says about this seventh power is very significant.

He must continue a short space (Revelation 17:10).

Since the papacy dominated the world scene for 1260 years, the longest period of any power in the history of this world, it could hardly be said that it continued "a short space"; thus this interpretation fails to meet the specific criteria given in the prophecy.

The reason that interpretations such as those cited above have failed to meet the specifications of the prophecy is because the setting of the prophecy has been overlooked. This prophecy was not fulfilled in the days of John the apostle; instead, it is fulfilled during the time of the end when the great investigative judgment is in session. We shall review this setting.

> And there came one of the seven angels which had the seven vials, and talked with me, saying unto me, Come hither; I will shew unto thee *the judgment* of the great whore that sitteth upon many waters (Revelation 17:1, emphasis added).

While it is not within the purpose of this book to examine the investigative judgment in detail, it should be stated that this judgment commenced in the year 1844.[1]

One recent attempt to unravel the mystery of the seven heads suggests that these represent popes. Commencing with Pope Pius XI, the pope who authorized the signing of the concordat with Mussolini in 1929, they number five who are fallen (the remaining four dead popes are Pius XII, John XXIII, Paul VI, and John Paul I). In this understanding, Pope John Paul II is advanced as the head that "is," and it is expected that he will die and be replaced by another pope who will sit on the papal throne for a·brief period. While interesting, such an explanation does not indicate why the period of the eighties is designated as the period that "is." The seven heads, or mountains, are seven powers. They are not specific rulers or forms of rule. Thus this view must be discarded.

Dr. Mervyn Maxwell (a modern exponent of prophecy), in his book, *God Cares*, correctly accepts the view that the sixth head, the head that "is," corresponds to the time of the investigative judgement. His interpretation of the seven heads consists of Babylon, Medo-Persia, Greece, Pagan Rome, Papal Rome, the wounded papacy, and the restored papacy. This view almost fulfills the given criteria, but not quite. It does not permit a reliable explanation of the mysterious eighth head; also, the wounded power of the papacy was so weak that it was in no position to strongly oppose God's truth; yet the prophecy does provide another vital clue to the correct understanding of this fascinating prophecy. We need to consider this.

> And the beast that was, and is not, even he is the eighth, and is of the seven, and goeth into perdition (Revelation 17:11).

The eighth is said to be a beast, and is reported to be of the seven beasts. This definitely directs our attention to the beasts that are so prominent in the prophecies of Daniel and Revelation.

With this information, our understanding of the prophecy is clarified. The first five beasts are as follows:

1. The lion with two eagle's wings, in Daniel 7:4, represented *Babylon*.

2. The bear that was raised on one side, in Daniel 7:5, represented *Medo-Persia*.

10:37 - 60

11:42 - 60

11:46 -

11:55 -

12:00 - 60

12:07 - 60

~~12:10~~

12:12 - 45

12:18 - 50

12:22 -

3. The four-headed leopard, in Daniel 7:6, represented *Greece*.

4. The ten-horned monster, in Daniel 7:7, represented *Pagan Rome*.

5. The seven-headed, ten-horned monster, in Revelation 13:1, 2, represented *Papal Rome*.

To this point, this understanding fits very comfortably with the characteristics that are set forth in this prophecy. Since Papal Rome received its deadly wound (Revelation 13:3) in 1798, we must search for another world power in Satan's master plan to oppose the church of God.

History concerning this era provides insight into the sixth head or beast—the one that "is." At the time of the dramatic fall of Papal Rome, one of the most bloodstained revolutions in history, the French Revolution was in progress. For the first time, the world was directed away from religion to atheism as the perpetrators of the French Revolution abolished religion and set up a profligate woman of low morals as the goddess of reason.

The influence of the movement of atheism was to have far-reaching effects upon the nations of Europe and beyond. Atheistic communism, which was to dominate Eastern Europe for over 70 years of the twentieth century, perceptively traced its roots to the French Revolution.

Karl Marx, the father of Communism, was a deep student of French history. He not only studied the French Revolution but also the revolution of 1848 in France, where civil war had broken out between the workers and the middle class. Marx wrote two books in German concerning the lessons to be learned from the French uprisings—*Die Klas-*

senkampfe in Frankreich 1848 bis 1850 and *Der Achtzehnte Brumaire des Louis Napoleon Bonaparte*. Even the nations of Western Europe were not untouched. Each, one by one, became a twentieth-century bastion for godlessness. Countries such as Italy and France possessed very strong communist parties. The Communist Party of Italy was capable of receiving 40 percent of the popular votes that were cast in democratic elections in 1948 (*Encyclopedia Britannica*, 1963 edition. Subject: communist parties). While we would not make an issue out of it, we do find it intriguing that the monster of Revelation 17 is designated by a color—a scarlet colored beast (Revelation 17:3). Could this be another specific clue inserted by an omniscient God in order to provide us evidence that the identity of this monster is atheistic communism? This power splashed its symbolic red across the nations of the earth.

Britain, a former bastion of Christianity, lost its way. An Englishman, Charles Darwin (about the time of the commencement of the investigative judgment), offered a theory of origins which discarded the concept of our Creator. Rationalists (such as the British earl, Bertram Russell) gathered much support. The English Church, in many instances, embraced agnosticism. Men such as Dr. Robinson, bishop of Woolwich, declared that it would be good to cease discussion about God in his absurd book, *Honest to God*. In a British broadcasting (BBC) television program, in the mid-eighties, Hugh Montefiore, bishop of Birmingham, was asked if he could present a sound piece of evidence for the existence of God. He suggested, "Well, there's evolution!" That same bishop, fifteen years earlier, had been accused of declaring Christ to be a homosexual, an accusation that he refused to deny.

Dr. David Perkins, bishop of Durham, declared that Christ was not born of a virgin birth, and that He was not resurrected from the dead. In 1985, a London *Daily Telegraph* survey of 42 Anglican bishops indicated that 31 expressed doubts in the resurrection of Christ.

> And if Christ be not risen, then is our preaching vain, and your faith is also vain (1 Corinthians 15:14).

Europe was not overwhelmed by a movement of religion; instead, it was overwhelmed by an avalanche of political and "religious" atheism.

Persecution of the loyal soldiers of Christ became almost as intense under this manifestation of satanic power as it had been under its predecessor, Papal Rome.

Undoubtedly, the beast of Revelation 17 includes atheism, both in the West and in the East, in the form of European communism. But this prophecy accurately predicted that it would not be the sixth head which would bring about the final satanic acts upon this earth. Just as the five previous powers had passed away, so communism and atheism, as the chief violators of the freedom of Christians to worship God by following biblical principles in the nineteenth and twentieth centuries, would also pass away.

In only a few months in 1989, the sixth head of atheistic communism has almost been swept away. The perceptive Christian has witnessed one of the most dramatic fulfillments of Bible prophecy as we enter the last decade of the second millennium of the Christian Era. The sixth head has fallen, the seventh is emerging; yet many Christians are blind to the significance of these events. We have been fully warned that the last days will come as a thief to the unprepared (1 Thessalonians 5:2).

> But ye, brethren, are not in darkness, that that day should overtake you as a thief. Ye are all the children of light, and the children of the day: we are not of the night, nor of darkness (1 Thessalonians 5:4, 5).

But are we? Many Christians are almost in a deep coma in regard to their perception of the signs of the times.

On January 15, 1990, Russell found himself seated next to an English Baptist pastor on a flight from London to Singapore. They discussed the cataclysmic events in the communist world. To Russell's surprise, he found that this minister of the gospel was totally oblivious to the great significance of the events which had just transpired. Apparently, he had not studied that vital book of Revelation.

Many atheists are not so blind. The renowned Marxist thinker, Milovan Djilas of Yugoslavia, made this insightful comment:

> The Soviets are changing the course of history, not just of Eastern Europe but of the world (Bombay, *Times of India*, January 29, 1990).

Djilas, while not aware of the scriptural basis of his assertion, nevertheless fully perceived the global significance of the fall of atheistic communism. As Christians, we possess infinitely more light than a Marxist philosopher.

The only beast which remains unaccounted for is the second beast of Revelation 13:11-17—the two horned lamblike beast which especially, but not exclusively, represents apostate Protestantism in the United States. This former pillar of religious tolerance, as we shall see, will change the established rights of its citizens and persecute God's saints during the process of restoring the power of Papal Rome.

> And he deceiveth them . . . saying to them that dwell on the earth, that they should make an image to the beast, which had the wound by a sword, and did live. And he had power to give life unto the image of the beast, that the image of the beast should both speak, and cause that as many as would not worship the image of the beast should be killed (Revelation 13:14, 15).

We have seen the effective demise of atheistic communism in Europe within the last quarter of the year 1989. Just as Medo-Persia followed Babylon without interval, Greece similarly followed Medo-Persia, and Pagan Rome succeeded Greece in rapid succession. Just as Papal Rome emerged from its pagan counterpart and atheism arose at the point of papal demise, we can also expect the rise of persecuting apostate Protestantism in the very near future because Satan leaves no vacuum in his unwearied efforts to defeat the gospel of Jesus. We have already seen Protestantism in the United States clamoring to restore the prestige and power of the Roman Catholic Church. Baptists, Lutherans, and others (discarding their Protestant heritage) are courting the favor of the papacy. The archbishop of Canterbury has joined the host of deluded religious leaders in blindly fulfilling divine prophecy. The papacy will soon be restored, with Protestant support, to its former position; then the following prophecy truly will be fulfilled.

Even he is the eighth, and is of the seven (Revelation 17:11),

The eighth is surely the restored papacy which was the fifth head of the seven.

Beware of the seventh and the eighth that it supports. Protestantism, in league with restored Catholicism, must continue a short space (Revelation 17:10).

Jesus is coming soon! Then this earth will be destroyed. We each need to ponder one awesome question:

> Seeing then that all these things shall be dissolved, what manner of persons ought ye to be in all holy conversation and godliness (2 Peter 3:11)?

God leaves us in no doubt concerning the answer to this all-important question.

> Wherefore, beloved, seeing that ye look for such things, be diligent that ye may be found of him in peace, without spot, and blameless (2 Peter 3:14).

We can be prepared for that great day only as we trust God's grace and power.

Endnote

[1] For a more biblical discussion of the investigative judgment and its prophetic dating, see *The Sacrificial Priest* by the same authors. Write to Hartland Publications, P.O. Box 1, Rapidan, Virginia 22733, U.S.A.

17

The Ten Horns

The prophecy of Revelation 17 presents another interesting international development. Referring to the ten horns which represent the nations of Europe, an explanation of their significance is provided.

> And the ten horns which thou sawest are ten kings, which have received no kingdom as yet; but receive power as kings one hour with the beast. These have one mind, and shall give their power and strength unto the beast (Revelation 17:12, 13).

The beast that is here referred to is not the red monster but, as the context of Revelation 17:11 demonstrates, it is the eighth beast—the papacy. Bible prophecy here informs us that the nations of Europe will, during the time of the seventh head, unite with the papacy to once more promote its authority; thus apostate Protestantism in the United States and the European nations will form a powerful alliance to promote papal dominance once more. We can anticipate that, as in the past, the papacy will take advantage of the power of the state to enforce fearful persecution of those who dare to stand against its evil doctrines. This persecution undoubtedly will surpass, in ferocity and intensity, the Inquisition of the Middle Ages. Remember that this eighth head (the restored papacy) will "cause that as many as would not worship the image of the beast should be killed" (Revelation 13:15).

The speech of John Paul II, April 1989, was ominous. Addressing thousands of young Italian soldiers, he expressed the hope "that each nation's army could one day be joined into a world authority" which would have the "effective means to enjoin respect for justice and the truth" (*Battle Cry*, summer 1989). There is no doubt that such a world army would enforce the ruthless dictates of the papacy against dissenters.

At the end of the sixth head (atheistic communism), the devil was immediately prepared with his seventh. American Protestantism and Protestantism elsewhere in this world are already loudly proclaiming a newfound unity of faith with Roman Catholicism. Similarly, Europe has been prepared for its role in the form of the European Economic Community which was established by the Treaty of Rome. Since the days of the Roman Empire, there has not been such close ties among the European nations. Twelve nations are already members—Belgium, Denmark, France, Greece, Ireland, Italy, Luxembourg, the Netherlands, Portugal, Spain, the United Kingdom, and West Germany. At the precise moment that Eastern Europe was throwing off the shackles of communism (October 1989), a most symbolic event happened in each of those 12 nations. This significant action was the abolition of national passports in those countries. Citizens of each of these 12 nations may now only obtain a common European passport.

Recently, another country has abandoned its tight restrictions:

> The Albanian People's Assembly last week granted all citizens the right to travel abroad, abolished restrictions on the practice of religion, and allowed all suspects the right to an attorney (*Time* magazine, May 21, 1990).

On December 31, 1992, closer unity will be forged in Europe. At that time, the nations of the European Economic Community will abolish all customs barriers across their borders. There will no longer be any immigration formalities when passing from one nation to the other. Thus these powers will be the United States of Europe except that there will not be full political unity. After December 31, 1992, it is proposed that the famous currencies of the past (the British pound sterling, the French franc, the German mark, the Italian lira, and the Dutch guilder) will all disappear in order to be replaced by a common currency known as the Eurodollar.

The United Kingdom is the only one of the 12 members in the Economic Community that holds any serious reservations to the implementation of the unified currency proposal. Mrs. Margaret Thatcher, prime minister of the United Kingdom, has always been halfhearted in her support of this European ideal. Significantly, her political fortunes have never been at a lower ebb than at the turn of the decade. Her political party was, in April 1990, over 20 percent behind the opposition Labor Party in opinion polls. Within her own party, moves are afoot to depose her from the party leadership. If this should transpire, the successor almost certainly would be Mr. Michael Heseltine. Contrast these two politicians.

> If Mrs. Thatcher is popularly seen as "anti-Europe," and is resisting British participation in the European monetary system because it would take away the sovereign right of parliament to decide Britain's economic policies, Mr. Heseltine tries to look as European as he can (Singapore *Straits Times*, March 20, 1990).

If Mrs. Thatcher resists the challenge to her leadership within the conservative party, she must face a general election before June 1992, just six months prior to the implementation of the unified monetary system and the elimination of immigration and customs barriers. At that election, she faces almost certain defeat. In either case, by December 31, 1992, it is almost certain that Margaret Thatcher, the last resistance to complete European unity, will be out of the political arena. All will be prepared for prophetic fulfillment.

Other European nations will surely seek entry into this powerful economic union. Four new nations are already seeking entry into the European Economic Community — Austria, Cyprus, Hungary, and Turkey (*Newsweek*, March 12, 1990). Others are expected to follow. There already is increasing cooperation between the EEC and other European nations. Six nations outside the EEC have formed the European Free Trade Association (EFTA). These are Austria, Finland, Iceland, Norway, Sweden, and Switzerland. A *Newsweek* report stated that "the odds are good that all six EFTA countries, including reluctant Switzerland, will have accepted close association with the community [the EEC] by the end of 1992.

Perhaps the unheralded 35-member Conference on Security and Cooperation in Europe (CSCE) is more significant. This organization consists of members from every European nation now that Albania has joined. This organization, which also includes the United States and Canada, was formed in 1975 by the Helsinki Final Act.

> The act remained largely a dead letter for the first decade after its adoption (*Newsweek,* March 12, 1990).

> To the surprise of most members, the CSCE debating club took on new life in the mid-1980s (by no coincidence) just as Gorbachev took power in Moscow (*Newsweek,* March 12, 1990) .

This was no coincidence because God had foretold that the nations of Europe would be of one mind at the time of the seventh head. Incredibly, *Newsweek* foresees that "the European Community and the CSCE are emerging as the likely poles around which the new Europe will organize itself."

The careful Bible student will studiously observe these two organizations, one a household name and the other almost unknown. The fact that the United States has a voice in the CSCE brings together the lamb-like beast and the ten horns as prophecy proclaims. These will uphold the papal power.

Since the days of the Roman Empire, Europe has never been in a position to speak as one mind. The CSCE represents the first organization in the history of Europe to which every European nation has excepted membership. In the light of Bible prophecy, this is most significant.

Newsweek was unaware that it was describing the fulfillment of prophecy when it reported that "the European Economic Community is tightening its political ties in order to 'speak as a single voice' in world affairs."

Now, for the first time in history, we have a single organization in which every European nation is a member, now that Albania officially joined. This is very significant in the fulfillment of Revelation 17.

> Albania yesterday edged further away from its self-imposed isolation after Mr. Adil Corcani, the prime minister, said that his country intended to join the all European Conference on Security and Cooperation in Europe (*Financial Times*, May 9, 1990).

In June 1990, Colin visited Copenhagen, Denmark. A meeting of the CSCE was in session. He attended the meeting, and observed every nation of Europe, from the Holy See (Vatican) to the U.S.S.R., present. Albania had sent representatives for the first time. The ominous significance of the growth of the CSCE may be judged by its evaluation by the Soviet Union.

> With the collapse of the Warsaw Pact & NATO insisting on incorporating a united Germany into the Western military alliance, Moscow is anxious to chart a new security system for Europe. . . . [Soviet foreign minister] Shevarnardze's idea is to convert the CSCE into what could be called a structure to safeguard European peace. . . . Here was the coalition of a greater European council grouping all the heads of the state that would meet once a year (Singapore *Straits Times*, June 1, 1990).

The CSCE would become the most powerful military alliance in the history of the world if the Soviet Union's suggestion is accepted.

While the "iron curtain" separated the two parts of Europe, this could not be so. Communism had to be dismantled before this prophecy could be fulfilled. As Mr. Gorbachev predicted, there will be "a commonwealth of independent nations pursuing one goal" (the *Australian Magazine*, February, 1990); thus the superstructure for the restoration of the eighth apostate power which was part of the seventh—the papacy—is already in place. As in the past, Satan has left no vacuum in his efforts, now so feverish, to subvert the faith of Christ.

Some have suggested that the brief alliance of the papacy and the united nations of Europe will endure for just 15 days because Scripture testifies that they "receive power as kings one hour with the beast" (Revelation 17:12).

One hour is one twenty fourth part of a day. Using prophetic symbolism, this would be equivalent to one twenty fourth part of a Jewish year (360 days), which is 15 days. The Greek word that is here translated as *one hour* sometimes implies *a brief period of time*; thus we cannot make a dogmatic statement about the duration of this unholy Roman alliance.

The nations of Europe will quickly see the folly of their action as the final events of earth's history unfold; however, it will then be forever too late. At that time, these nations will turn on the papacy with unprecedented ferocity.

> And the ten horns which thou sawest upon the beast, these shall hate the whore, and shall make her

desolate and naked, and shall eat her flesh, and burn her with fire. For God hath put in their hearts to fulfil his will, and to agree, and give their kingdom unto the beast, until the words of God shall be fulfilled. And the woman which thou sawest is that great city [Rome], which reigneth over the kings of the earth (Revelation 17:16-18).

Before the end of April 1990, led by President Francois Mitterrand, of France, and Chancellor Helmut Kohl, of West Germany, the 12 nations of the European Economic Community were launched on a pathway toward political union. Their objective is to unify a common foreign and security policy by 1993. Such an achievement would lead the European Community of nations toward political unity. This was always in the minds of the early architects of the EEC, but few believed that this was possible. Though Great Britain, Denmark, and Portugal expressed reservations and concerns about this direction, these concerns were not sufficient to dampen the enthusiasm of the majority of nations (Washington *Post*, April 29, 1990).

It is hard to project the impact of such a momentous decision. The Word of God clearly states that complete political union of these nations cannot be achieved, as we have seen (see chapter, entitled "European Political Unity"). The prophet, Daniel, in his interpretation of the dream of King Nebuchadnezzar, foretold the collapse of the Babylonian kingdom and the subsequent rise and fall of Medo-Persia, Greece, and Rome (Daniel 2:36-40). The Roman Empire was not to be succeeded by another world political power; instead, it was to collapse into the ten divisions which represented most of Europe. These ten divisions will never be united until the Lord sets up His kingdom.

> And whereas thou sawest iron mixed with miry clay, they shall mingle themselves with the seed of men: but they shall not cleave one to another, even as iron is not mixed with clay. And in the days of these kings shall the God of heaven set up a kingdom, which shall never be destroyed: and the kingdom shall not be left to other people, but it shall break in pieces and consume all these kingdoms, and it shall stand for ever (Daniel 2:43, 44).

It is clear that there will be an intimate union as the nations of Europe unite together in "one mind" in order to serve the objectives of the papacy, but Daniel's prophecy assures us that this union will fall short of political intergration.

> And the ten horns which thou sawest are ten kings, which have received no kingdom as yet; but receive power as kings one hour with the beast. These have one mind, and shall give their power and strength unto the beast (Revelation 17:12, 13).

The stunning events in Europe not only confirm Bible prophecy but give unmistakable evidence of the soon return of Jesus. Many will be shocked to learn that the European Economic Community in Europe has chosen the tower of Babel as its symbol and "Many Peoples, One Voice" as its motto.

Undoubtedly, every effort will be made to suppress efforts that expose the papacy. Politicians in Great Britain are already talking of changing the blasphemy laws to cover materials that stir up religious hatred. Such laws would easily be applied to those who call men and women out of the papacy.

As we observe these movements rapidly transpiring before our very eyes,[1] we need to press close to our God. Each must unreservedly dedicate his or her life to Jesus.

> That ye may be blameless and harmless, the sons of God, without rebuke, in the midst of a crooked and perverse nation, among whom ye shine as lights in the world (Philippians 2:15).

Endnote

[1] One puzzling aspect of this prophecy is its comment concerning the kings that have received no kingdom as yet (Revelation 17:12). This may refer to the fact that the union of these European states would not lead to a political unity. Note that the word "kingdom" is in the singular. Another less likely interpretation is that other monarchies will be restored as the Spanish monarchy was at the time of the death of General Franco. A surprising number of monarchies are still functioning in Europe, including half of the members of the European Economic Community—Belgium, Denmark, Luxembourg, the Netherlands, Spain, and the United Kingdom. Other monarchies in Europe are to be found in Liechtenstein, Monaco, Norway, and Sweden. The collapse of communism has raised the hopes of many claimants to the former thrones of Europe. *Life* magazine, March 1990, quoted King Michael of Romania as saying, "If they want me back, of course I will go. As constitutional monarch, I can guarantee the constitution, freedom, democracy." Several other deposed kings and descendants of such kings were cited to have similar desires. These included Grand Duke Vladimir, of Russia; Germany's Louis Ferdinand, of Prussia; Crown Prince Alexander, of Yugoslavia; Otto, archduke of the Austro-Hun-

garian Empire; King Simon II, of Bulgaria; King Constantine II, of Greece; and King Leka I, of Albania. Others in France and Italy covet a return to a monarchial system.

18

The Final Fate of the Antichrist

We have noted that the nations of Europe will finally turn upon the papacy with great ferocity (Revelation 17:16); however, before this occurs, Scripture states that the nations of the world will cry, "Peace and safety" (1 Thessalonians 5:3).

Cries of peace are already being heard. These cries are based upon two diplomatic negotiations in Rome and Moscow.

> The pope's vision of a unified Europe from the Atlantic to the Urals and Mr. Mikhail Gorbachev's notion of a "common European house" had, until recently, only geography in common. Yet the more the Soviet leader introduces changes in his country and reorients Soviet foreign policy, the closer they grow (Singapore *Straits Times*, March 13, 1990).

It is the Vatican which is largely orchestrating those changes in Soviet foreign policy.

The word in Rome is that, during the meetings with Mr. Gorbachev in December, the pope noted that there had not been bloodshed in the Baltic Republic [Lithuania], the Ukraine, or the other Soviet regions where there is a strong Roman Catholic presence. This was in striking contrast to what was happening in mostly Muslim Azerbaijan. The message to the Soviet leader seemed to be that Mr. Gorbachev could survive the secession of the Baltic states and even periodic trouble in Central Asia. But if turmoil erupted in the important, populous Ukraine, he could not survive. Because of the large Catholic population there, the Vatican could provide invaluable help in keeping spirits calm. The pope said, after Mr. Gorbachev's visit, that he would pray for the Soviet leader. Mr. Gorbachev said that he had asked for the pope's spiritual contribution. The design is one of vast proportions. For Mr. Gorbachev, it would mean substantial help in keeping order and stability in the sensitive regions of his country where there are large numbers of Catholics. For the pope, it would mean gaining religious freedom in the Soviet Union (*Straits Times*, March 13, 1990).

Past indications are that promises made by the Vatican are only valid so long as they meet Vatican political needs. When expedient to do so, the Vatican regards its assurances as ropes of sand broken with ease; thus Gorbachev, in accepting John Paul II's promise to keep Roman Catholics in the Ukraine calm, would be a naive student of Vatican political policy if he expected an indefinite tenure to that promise.

If Lithuanian independence is firmly established and recognized by the world community of nations, it would not be beyond Vatican treachery for it to encourage similar ambitions in the Ukraine. Already, mild calls for such independence are abroad.

> The Ukrainian nationalist party, Rukh, buoyed by fresh election victories after just six months in existence, has pledged to follow the example of the Baltic states and push for independence (Bangkok *Nation*, March 22, 1990).

Fortunately, for the U.S.S.R., the Rukh Party obtained only 30 percent of the seats in the first multiparty election; thus, at the present, it does not possess the political muscle to implement its agenda.

Mr. Odarich, the leader of the Rukh Party, has made an ominous prediction:

> Against little Lithuania, he [Gorbachev] could still find a pretext to send in troops. But, against the Ukrainian people, this is impossible (*ibid.*).

The devout student of prophecy will watch the events in the U.S.S.R. with great interest as they evolve, particularly the interplay between the Kremlin and the Vatican.

While all three Baltic republics—Estonia, Latvia, and Lithuania—crave their pre-1940 independence, it is quite significant that Lithuania, with its more than 80 percent Roman Catholic population, was the first to declare its independence. The other two have cautiously followed. This turn of events did not provide a simple solution for Gorbachev. Military intervention was hardly a viable option because of the delicate Vatican relations at stake. On the other hand, doing nothing would have been an invitation for other republics to follow the same example. Gorbachev chose the less dangerous option of economic boycott—a warning to other Soviet republics; yet this option is less threatening to developing relations with the Vatican.

Significantly, on March 15, 1990, the Vatican and the U.S.S.R exchanged ambassadors for the first time in over 70 years.

We can rest assured that it is not religious freedom that the Vatican seeks for the U.S.S.R. Prophecy predicts that papal dominance will be achieved in the U.S.S.R. and throughout Europe, but only for a "short space." As the iron curtain totally crumbles and becomes only a matter of historical interest, the cries of peace are perfectly understandable. Troops and armaments in Europe have been increasingly cut back; nevertheless, the same divine voice declared that there would be a swift end to peace.

> For when they shall say, Peace and safety; then sudden destruction cometh upon them, as travail upon a woman with child; and they shall not escape (1 Thessalonians 5:3).

This depicts the cataclysmic end to the powers of this earth, when God's hand is felt in the affairs of men. The nations of the world have followed, for too long, the policies of expediency instead of righteousness. The final support (in Europe, America, and the whole world) of the antichrist power is the final affront to a pure and holy God.

In a few brief verses, the prophet, Daniel, saw the scenario which we have portrayed. A little background detail is necessary. At the death of Alexander the Great, his kingdom was divided into four parts by his four powerful generals. Lysimachus became the king of the North; Ptolemy because the king of the South; Cassander accepted the throne of the Western territories, and Seleucus, the Eastern.

Daniel used the terms, *King of the North* and *King of the South*, to depict the principal powers that are involved in the last-day events which have been discussed in this book. We know that they are last-day events because Daniel places them "at the time of the end" (Daniel 11:40). Let us read this fascinating prophecy:

> And at the time of the end shall the king of the south push at him [the king of the north]: and the king of the north shall come against him like a whirlwind, with chariots, and with horsemen, and with many ships; and he shall enter into the countries, and shall overflow and pass over (Daniel 11:40).[1]

Two victories are recorded here. Firstly, the king of the South, at the time of the end, "pushes at" the king of the North. Secondly, the king of the North eventually gets his revenge, and destroys the king of the South with great alacrity ("like a whirlwind"). The present day kings of the South and the North, as symbolized, are not geographical entities; instead, they are political entities that possess characteristics of the two former kingdoms.

This fact is easily illustrated in examination of the king of the South. The original king of the South incorporated the territory of Egypt. No ancient kingdom blasphemed the name of God more than this land did. Pharaoh retorted when Moses and Aaron sought the release of the Israelites from Egypt.

> And Pharaoh said, who is the Lord, that I should obey his voice to let Israel go? I know not the Lord, neither will I let Israel go (Exodus 5:2).

Egypt symbolized atheism, and was a fitting symbol of its political entity—communism. Another beast, the beast of Revelation 11, was appropriately represented by Sodom and Egypt (Revelation 11:8), two areas over which the king of the South ruled. This is the least noticed beast in the book of Revelation; yet it is a powerful symbol of the atheism that commenced at the time of the French Revolution.

It is advantageous to spend a brief moment examining this beast because it clarifies a number of things about the king of the South. In Revelation, chapter 11, God's two witnesses—the Old and New Testaments—are mentioned. The zealous effort to destroy these witnesses during the era of papal dominance is outlined. But, with the coming of the sixteenth-century Reformation, the power of those witnesses was seen.

> And when they [the Old and New Testaments] shall have finished their testimony, the beast that ascendeth out of the bottomless pit shall make war against them, and shall overcome them, and kill them (Revelation 11:7).

This passage refers to the banning of the Scriptures in Paris and throughout France during the French Revolution. At that time, thousands of copies of the Holy Bible were cast into the bonfires.

> And their dead bodies shall lie in the street of the great city, which spiritually is called Sodom and Egypt, where also our Lord was crucified (Revelation 11:8).

> It all started in Poland, say close advisers to the pope. One can hardly deny it, adds Adam Bonlecki [a priest], editor of the Polish edition of *Osservatore*

Romano. During Karol Wojtyla's first trip to Poland as Pope John Paul II, in 1979, the streets were filled with millions of people. He sent a clear message to the crowds, "Liberate yourselves from fear; it is the only tool the regime can use against you." That was the beginning of the great events that unfolded in the following years, says Bishop Szczepan Wesoly, who accompanied the pope. For the first time, the people realized the extent of their potential strength. A year later, during the strikes at the Lenin Shipyards, in Gdansk, huge portraits of the pope were everywhere, a new and incredible thing in a communist country— the snowball that became an avalanche. And now Vatican diplomats, some of the world's most effective, are on the move (Singapore *Straits Times*, March 13, 1990).

God's Word has surely been fulfilled because the papacy has overflowed and surpassed the strength of communism. And this has transpired as we have looked on.

The ascendancy of the papacy, with its period of terrible persecution, will be mercifully short-lived.

The ten horns [nations of Europe] which thou sawest upon the beast, these shall hate the whore, and shall make her desolate and naked, and shall eat her flesh, and burn her with fire (Revelation 17:16).

Daniel, too, predicts the same fate for the papacy, but uses different words. Daniel declares that the king of the North "shall come to his end, and none shall help him" (Daniel 11:45).

The antichrist will finally be abhorred by all the nations which supported her in the time of her ascendancy. But it will be forever too late for those who supported the papacy when it was a popular movement. Such heeded man's dictates instead of responding to the pleas of a loving God. Today is the moment to make our calling and election sure. It will be forever too late for those who await the destruction of the papacy before they turn to God. Let us always cherish God's promise to us:

> The Lord is not slack concerning his promise, as some men count slackness; but is longsuffering to usward, not willing that any should perish, but that all should come to repentance (2 Peter 3:9).

Endnote

[1] Pastor Jan Knopper presented an excellent exposition of this passage in Sydney, Australia, in December 1990.

19

Future Expectations

What can the faithful student of prophecy expect to take place between now and the return of Jesus? What role will the papacy play in these events?

Revelation and Daniel both depict the papacy as a persecuting power.

I beheld, and the same horn made war with the saints, and prevailed against them (Daniel 7:21).

And he shall speak great words against the most High, and shall wear out the saints of the most High (Daniel 7:25).

And it was given unto him to make war with the saints, and to overcome them: and power was given him over all kindreds, and tongues, and nations (Revelation 13:7).

And he had power to give life unto the image of the beast, that the image of the beast should both speak, and cause that as many as would not worship the image of the beast should be killed (Revelation 13:15).

>And that no man might buy or sell, save he that
>had the mark, or the name of the beast, or the number
>of his name (Revelation 13:17).

>And I saw the woman drunken with the blood of
>the saints, and with the blood of the martyrs of Jesus
>(Revelation 17:6).

This persecution is directed toward the true followers of
God. In recent years, the religious and political climates
have not been as conducive, as in past ages, to persecution.
But religious groups, step by step, will give their allegiance
to the papacy. As nation after nation recognizes the papacy
as the great cohesive force in the world, the religious and
political climates are being altered. Persecution of God's
faithful people will follow. This persecution will be accepted as an appropriate weapon against those who will
have nothing to do with a religious ecumenism that has
been established upon apostasy. Let us not forget that the
Roman Catholic Church has never officially repented of the
grave evils that it perpetrated against God's saints during
the Middle Ages.

Once again, the state will execute the dictates of the
church. As history repeats itself, we can expect this union
of church and state to exercise persecution and terror upon
faithful Christians. The forces which are presently advocating church/state unity are already strong in the United
States. Sadly, its own statements make it clear that, when
the circumstances are right, the Roman Catholic Church
will again resort to ruthless persecution. In the nineteenth
century, the archbishop of Saint Louis shared his conviction and purpose concerning his clerical duties:

> Heresy and unbelief are crimes; and in Christian countries, as in Italy and Spain, for instance, where all the people are Catholics, and where the Catholic religion is a central part of the law of the land, they are punished as other crimes.
>
> Every cardinal, archbishop, and bishop of the Catholic Church takes an oath of allegiance to the pope, in the following words: "Heretics, schismatics, and rebels to our said lord [the pope], or his aforesaid successors, I will to my utmost persecute and oppose" (nineteenth-century archbishop).

God's authentic people will increasingly depend upon Christ alone for their strength and courage. The Word of God will provide the sole foundation for their faith and practice. They will cling to the Lord for strength to gain victory over every deceptive art of the evil one. They will be sanctified by the truth. With all other faithful people, they will receive the divine power of the latter rain, which will enable them to take the gospel of the soon-coming Saviour to every individual upon the earth.

> Then shall we know, if we follow on to know the Lord: his going forth is prepared as the morning; and he shall come unto us as the rain, as the latter and former rain unto the earth (Hosea 6:3).
>
> And it shall come to pass afterward, that I will pour out my spirit upon all flesh; and your sons and your daughters shall prophesy, your old men shall dream dreams, your young men shall see visions (Joel 2:28).

At the time of Pentecost, the apostles received the former rain.

> And when the day of Pentecost was fully come, they were all with one accord in one place. And suddenly there came a sound from heaven as of a rushing

mighty wind, and it filled all the house where they were sitting. And there appeared unto them cloven tongues like as of fire, and it sat upon each of them. And they were all filled with the Holy Ghost, and began to speak with other tongues, as the Spirit gave them utterance (Acts 2:1-4).

This power enabled the early Christians to take the gospel to all parts of the world. Writing about A.D. 64, Paul was able to report that the gospel had, in just three decades, spread worldwide.

If ye continue in the faith grounded and settled, and be not moved away from the hope of the gospel, which ye have heard, and *which was preached to every creature which is under heaven*; whereof I Paul am made a minister . . . (Colossians 1:23, emphasis added).

The latter rain will give power to God's faithful remnant to take the message of Christ's soon coming to every part of the planet. The gospel that will be preached worldwide will be the everlasting gospel.

And I saw another angel fly in the midst of heaven, having the everlasting gospel to preach unto them that dwell on the earth, and to every nation, and kindred, and tongue, and people, saying with a loud voice, Fear God, and give glory to him; for the hour of his judgment is come: and worship him that made heaven, and earth, and the sea, and the fountains of waters (Revelation 14:6, 7).

This gospel (see chapter 22, entitled "Come Out of Her My People") will be especially directed toward the faithful who are presently in the Roman Catholic Church and those Protestant churches who have surrendered their allegiance to the papacy. But it will also spread to every non-Christian land.

> And I heard another voice from heaven, saying,
> Come out of her, my people, that ye be not partakers
> of her sins, and that ye receive not of her plagues. For
> her sins have reached unto heaven, and God hath
> remembered her iniquities (Revelation 18:4, 5).

At that time, all the world will be emphasizing unity (political, economic, social, and religious), and the papacy is seen as the great peacemaker and leader in social justice. The efforts of God's faithful people to call His people out of Babylon will be seen as divisive, disruptive, and counterproductive to worldwide peace initiatives. This small, scattered group of faithful will increasingly become the object of examination by the enemies of truth. After all efforts to "convert" them to papal allegiance fails, state-administered persecution will be directed against them. This is the witness of prophecy. No doubt, this action will be defended by claiming that the saints alone are responsible for the failure to achieve total peace and unity upon the earth. They will be represented as traitors. The efforts of the faithful to convince the masses that biblical truth alone is the foundation of true Christianity and genuine peace will prove futile.

All except the most sincere will reject the pleas of the faithful, and will turn their wrath against them because most are biblically illiterate and drunk with the false beliefs of the papacy. The masses will not have the least thought that they are rejecting the final invitation of a loving, longsuffering Saviour. By their actions, they will reject God's law. In so doing, they reject the One of whom the law is the very transcript of His character.

It is self-evident that the day of worship will provide the central issue in this final test of loyalty to God. The Scriptures foretell that this false church will attempt to change the times that God had established. The only time of worship that God has perpetually established is the Sabbath.

> And he [the little-horn power] shall speak great words against the most High, and shall wear out the saints of the most High, and *think to change times and laws* (Daniel 7:25, emphasis added).

It is certain that no human authority can change God's law or His ordained time for worship. The papacy has succeeded in convincing most of the Christian church that it has that authority; thus it is not surprising that the Roman Catholic Church has long boasted that its claim to church authority is superior to biblical authority. Her claim is that her power is vested in the change of Sabbath worship from Saturday to Sunday observance. Here are a few examples:

> **Question:** *Which is the Sabbath day?*
>
> **Answer:** Saturday is the Sabbath day.
>
> **Question:** *Why do we observe Sunday instead of Saturday?*
>
> **Answer:** We observe Sunday instead of Saturday because the Catholic Church transferred the solemnity from Saturday to Sunday (Peter Geiermann, *The Convert's Catechism of Catholic Doctrine*, 1977 edition, p. 50).
>
> **Question:** *Have you any other way of proving that the church has power of instituting festivals or precepts?*
>
> **Answer:** Had she not had such power, she could not have done that in which all modern religionists agree with her. She could not have substituted the observance of Sunday, the first day of the week, for the

> observance of Saturday, the seventh day, a change for
> which there is no scriptural authority (Stephen
> Keenan, *A Doctrinal Catechism*, 1876, p. 174).

The Roman Catholic Church has always claimed the
homage of the Protestant churches because of their observance of Sunday as their day of worship.

> It was the Catholic Church which, by the body of
> Jesus Christ, has transferred this rest to the Sunday in
> remembrance of our Lord; thus, the observance of
> Sunday by the Protestants is a homage they pay, in
> spite of themselves, to the authority of the [Catholic]
> church (Louis Gaston de Segur, *Plain Talk About the
> Protestantism of Today*, 1868, p. 225).

> The Catholic Church for over 1,000 years before the
> existence of a Protestant, by virtue of her divine mis
> sion, changed the day from Saturday to Sunday. . . .

> But, the Protestant says, "How can I receive the
> teachings of an apostate church? How, we ask, have
> you managed to receive her teaching all your life, *in
> direct opposition* to your recognized teacher, the Bible,
> on the Sabbath question" ("The Christian Sabbath,"
> from *The Catholic Mirror*, 1893, pp. 29-31)?

It is true that the Roman Catholic Church has instituted
many other nonbiblical practices; for example, the rosary,
penance, purgatory, limbo, and infant baptism are Roman
Catholic innovations that are not founded upon the Word
of God. But none of these have assumed the symbolic importance to papal authority that the change of the Sabbath
has achieved. The Sabbath has become the basis upon
which the papal church has established its authority above
the authority of the inspired Word of Scripture. This
should not be surprising because the Sabbath was established as God's special sign of authority. It establishes the

fact that Christ is our Creator. By worshiping on His Sabbath, we accept His sovereignty in our lives. By rejecting the Sabbath, the Roman Catholic Church has rejected the Lord of the Sabbath (Mark 2:28).

All sorts of spurious arguments have been used in a vain effort to sustain Sunday sacredness. Some have attributed the "solemnity" of Sunday to the fact that Christ rose from the dead on that day. But Jesus instituted only two ordinances of the church to commemorate His resurrection—baptism (Romans 6:3-8) and the communion service (1 Corinthians 11:23-26). Christ never inferred that Sunday should be observed in place of the Sabbath. The pagan origin of Sunday observance is clearly recognized by the fact that the first day of the week, Sunday, is observed from midnight to midnight, a practice that was instituted by the pagans (instead of observing the divine time schedule from sundown to sundown). We could properly ask the Christian world why it did not instead choose Friday as its day of worship, as our Lord died on that day. In 1985, the London *Daily Telegraph* reported that 31, of the 42, Anglican bishops that were surveyed did not believe in Christ's resurrection. It would be most difficult for these bishops to argue Sunday sacredness as the basis of a resurrection in which they did not believe.

The Bible emphasizes that the Sabbath seal is central to God's seal of loyalty that will be placed in the foreheads of God's final faithful people.

> Saying, Hurt not the earth, neither the sea, nor the trees, till we have sealed the servants of our God in their foreheads (Revelation 7:3).

> And I looked, and, lo, a Lamb stood on the mount
> Sion, and with him an hundred forty and four
> thousand, having his Father's name written in their
> foreheads (Revelation 14:1).

Scripture specifies that the Sabbath is the sign of
sanctification.

> Speak thou also unto the children of Israel, saying,
> Verily my sabbaths ye shall keep: for it is a sign be-
> tween me and you throughout your generations; that
> ye may know that I am the Lord that doth sanctify
> you (Exodus 31:13).

> Moreover also I gave them my sabbaths, to be a
> sign between me and them, that they might know that
> I am the Lord that sanctify them (Ezekiel 20:12).

In the Bible, the sign of God is synonymous with the seal
of God.

> And he received the *sign* of circumcision, a *seal* of
> the righteousness of faith which he had yet being un-
> circumcised (Romans 4:11, emphasis added).

Those who will be God's loyal people at the end-time
will be Sabbathkeepers. The Word of God is clear that
these end-time saints will be keepers of the law, irrespective of persecution, deprivation, and death threats.

> And the dragon was wroth with the woman, and
> went to make war with the remnant of her seed,
> which *keep the commandments of God*, and have the tes-
> timony of Jesus Christ (Revelation 12:17, emphasis
> added).

> Here is the patience of the saints: here are they that
> *keep the commandments of God*, and the faith of Jesus
> (Revelation 14:12, emphasis added).

> Blessed are they that *do his commandments*, that they
> may have right to the tree of life, and may enter in

through the gates into the city (Revelation 22:14, emphasis added).

God's true saints who are faithful unto death will keep
all God's commandments in the divine strength that is
provided by Christ. These saints will live eternally with
Him.

20

The Mark of the Beast and the Seal of God

Although the Bible states that the saints will receive the seal of God that secures their eternal salvation, it also introduces the mark of the beast, which will be received by those who reject the invitation of Christ to separate from Babylon. This mark will be received either in the forehead or in the hand.

> And he causeth all, both small and great, rich and poor, free and bond, to receive a mark in their right hand, or in their foreheads (Revelation 13:16).

> And the third angel followed them, saying with a loud voice, If any man worship the beast and his image, and receive his mark in his forehead, or in his hand . . . (Revelation 14:9).

Some students of Scripture have postulated that lost men and women will receive a visible mark; however, in view of the symbolic language of Revelation, it is evident that the mark, or seal, that is received in the forehead is indicative of allegiance to Satan or Christ. These marks will be embedded in the mind, the decision-making area of the brain. Those who receive the mark in the hand (unlike those who receive it in the forehead) will not be deceived by the papal power or its false teachings; however, they will capitulate when the test comes. They will obey the dictates of the antichrist and fail to secure eternal life because of their refusal to fully accept Jesus and all His directions in their lives. The following words of Jesus are of eternal importance to every Christian:

> Then said Jesus unto his disciples, If any man will come after me, let him deny himself, and take up his cross, and follow me. For whosoever will save his life shall lose it: and whosoever will lose his life for my sake shall find it. For what is a man profited, if he shall gain the whole world, and lose his own soul? or what shall a man give in exchange for his soul? For the Son of man shall come in the glory of his Father with his angels; and then he shall reward every man according to his works (Matthew 16:24-27).

This certainly is the time to draw close to Jesus, allowing Him to lead in every step of our lives.

We can expect that, in its last, desperate effort to subjugate the whole world to its nefarious deception, step by determined step, the papacy will attempt to enforce Sunday observance as a sign of its authority and power. Because of the prophesied allegiance of the nations to the papacy (see Revelation 14:8, 18:3), there will be a repetition of the past—the civil governments of the world will enforce the wishes of the papacy; thus national and international laws will be framed, requiring all to worship on Sunday. It can be expected that legislation will eventually be enacted, in an attempt to force Sabbathkeepers to violate God's sacred day of worship.

A careful study of Revelation, chapter 13, indicates that the United States will play a significant role in these closing events. As we have seen, the prophecy of Revelation 13 identifies the second power that will play the primary role as the enforcer of the dictates of the papacy. This new power is brought to view in the second part of Revelation 13.

> And I beheld another beast coming up out of the earth; and he had two horns like a lamb, and he spake as a dragon (Revelation 13:11).

The following facts demonstrate that this power is the United States of America.

1. A beast in biblical prophecy always represents an earthly power. This is evident from Daniel's prophecy of the four beasts.

> And four great beasts came up from the sea, diverse one from another. The first was like a lion, and had eagle's wings: I beheld till the wings thereof were plucked, and it was lifted up from the earth, and made stand upon the feet as a man, and a man's heart was given to it. And behold another beast, a second, like to a bear, and it raised up itself on one side, and it had three ribs in the mouth of it between the teeth of it: and they said thus unto it, Arise, devour much flesh. After this I beheld, and lo another, like a leopard, which had upon the back of it four wings of a fowl; the beast had also four heads; and dominion was given to it. After this I saw in the night visions, and behold a fourth beast, dreadful and terrible, and strong exceedingly; and it had great iron teeth: it devoured and brake in pieces, and stamped the

residue with the feet of it: and it was diverse from all
the beasts that were before it; and it had ten horns
(Daniel 7:3-7).

These four beasts represented the four successive
dominant political powers of Babylon, Medo-Persia,
Greece, and Rome.

2. This new power, revealed in Revelation 13:11, arose
from the earth. It will be noted that the powers of Daniel 7
arose from the sea.

And four great beasts came up from the *sea*, diverse
one from another (Daniel 7:3, emphasis added).

The *sea*, in biblical prophecy, represents multitudes and
people.

And he saith unto me, The waters which thou
sawest, where the whore sitteth, are peoples, and multitudes, and nations, and tongues (Revelation 17:15).

These powers that are depicted in Daniel, chapter 7,
arose out of the densely populated areas of the Old World.
This new power, by contrast, must be a New World nation
because it arises from the earth (indicating a sparsely populated area) instead of the sea.

3. This second beast power had to arise around 1798 (the
end of the 1260 years of European papal domination).
Prophecy spoke about the first beast of Revelation 13 which
represented the papacy.

And there was given unto him a mouth speaking
great things and blasphemies; and power was given
unto him to continue forty and two months [or 1260
days] (Revelation 13:5).

The lamb-like beast arose to power after the papal beast, thus fixing its origin in the latter portion of the eighteenth century.

4. This new power is depicted as lamb-like in its beginning; whereas, the other beasts of biblical prophecy are generally depicted as beasts of prey. Such a power would establish itself without great conquest in a minimally populated region of the world.

5. The choice of a lamb rather than a sheep indicates a very young nation.

The biblical criteria excludes every nation upon earth except the United States of America. It arose under the banner of a constitution which granted, as no other nation before, political and religious liberty. In this enactment, the United States forged the peaceable characteristics of a lamb. It arose, at the end of the eighteenth century, in the sparsely populated territory of the New World that is far removed from the denser populated nations of Europe and the Middle East. When the United States gained independence, its total population was a mere three million.

Divine prophecy predicted that the characteristics of this lamb-like beast would change. It would speak as a dragon; thus we must expect the United States to become, even though founded upon the principles of religious freedom, an oppressive power that will enforce papal dictates.

Recent court rulings indicate a dramatic departure from the time-honored American heritage of protecting the religious rights of minority groups. A 1990 Sepreme Court opinion (in the United States) is a frightening example of this.

In what was called a "radical departure" from previous rulings protecting religion, the Supreme Court Tuesday forcefully declared that it would no longer shield believers whose practices violate general laws.

Religions that are out of the mainsteam are most likely to be affected because their unconventional practices and lack of political clout have led them to depend on the courts for protection.

The ruling came in the case of two American Indians who were fired from their jobs as drug counselors, in Oregon, after they admitted ingesting peyote during a religious ceremony. On a 6-3 vote, the court upheld their dimissal.

But in the sweeping opinion, Justice Antonin Scalia went far beyond the case, and declared that when religious rights clash with the government's need for reform rules, the court will side with the government.

As a nation, "we cannot afford the luxury" of striking down laws simply because they limit someone's religious practices, Scalia said. He advised religious adherents to look to the political system, not the courts for protection ("Religious Fine Print Blurred," *The Fresno Bee,* April 18, 1990).

When the supreme court of Nebraska, in 1990, ruled that a Jehovah Witness father could not teach his daughter Jehovah Witness beliefs in competition to his divorced wife's Roman Catholic beliefs, another nail was hammered into the coffin of religious liberty.

And he exerciseth all the power of the first beast before him, and causeth the earth and them which dwell therein to worship the first beast, whose deadly wound was healed (Revelation 13:12).

Sadly, we must expect that this great nation of freedom will be transformed into a persecuting power whose main object will be to obliterate God's saints from the earth.

> And he causeth all, both small and great, rich and poor, free and bond, to receive a mark in their right hand, or in their foreheads: And that no man might buy or sell, save he that had the mark, or the name of the beast, or the number of his name (Revelation 13:16, 17).

> And he had power to give life unto the image of the beast, that the image of the beast should both speak, and cause that as many as would not worship the image of the beast should be killed (Revelation 13:15).

Is it not highly significant that members of the Protestant churches of America are now seeking reconciliation with the Roman Catholic Church? Even one of the most conservative of all Protestant churches in the United States, the Southern Baptists, seeks basic agreement with the Roman Catholic Church. (See chapter 9, entitled "All That Dwell Upon the Earth Shall Worship Him.")

The Southern Baptists are not the only Protestants who are drawing closer to Roman Catholics.

> Roman Catholics and Lutherans stepped closer together Monday, when church officials from both denominations announced plans to draw up a covenant that will increase cooperation between the most powerful religious bodies in Minnesota (The Minneapolis *Star and Tribune*, Oct. 17 1989).

> The capitulation of Protestantism to Catholicism is seen worldwide. In July 1990, the president of the Australasian Council of Churches, the Anglican bishop of Bendigo, Bishop Oliver Heywood, and the Roman Catholic archbishop of Sidney, Cardinal Ed-

ward Clancy, sat side by side, in Adelaide, talking about plans for a new national ecumenical body. . . . The move has been described as "a revolution" in Anglican-Catholic nations, and could be the first step towards the eventual merger of the two churches (Sidney *Morning Herald,* July 1990).

The new ecumenical body is projected to be operating by 1992. It seems that the 1992-1993 era will be tremendously significant in the fulfillment of Bible prophecy. Ninety percent of the Christian community, in Australia, will be represented in the new organization.

The following assertion is even more ominous:

Its [the new ecumenical council's] formation is also expected to encourage the church community to take an even greater part in the political area. "Politics is what drives our society in many ways, and if the church is to be part of society, which it is, then clearly we have to be involved," Bishop Heyward said. "If there is a bit of rough and tumble, then so be it" (Sidney *Morning Herald*).

When the church unites with the state, persecution of dissenters inevitably follows.

Today many Christians of various faiths and their ministers are joining together in special days of prayer for Christian unity, little recognizing that such prayers do not ascend to God, but to the archdeciever. At these ecumenical prayer meetings, Christians are being subtly conditioned to unite with Rome.

It is obvious that not only the churches of Protestantism are turning their faces toward Rome but also the nations of the world are uniting under the supervision of the papacy. We can expect these unions to continue to accelerate their cooperation in the near future. The closer they come together; the more secure this unity will be achieved. The persecution of God's people will consequently follow this renewed union of church and state. The Bible predicts it. History confirms that this has always been the result of such a union. The gospel will be taken to every part of the world under these most difficult and trying circumstances. Many faithful children of Christ will lose their lives during this time.

Communist nations have officially apoligized for their past wrongs. Poland and East Germany have openly apoligized for joining the Russian Army in quelling the democracy movement in Prague during 1968. Even the U.S.S.R. has at last confessed its guilt to Poland for the liquidation of 15,570 officers of the Polish Army in the Katyn Forest in 1940. Even the emperor of Japan, in 1990, apoligized for the actions of Imperial Japan against Korea during its occupation in the years of 1905-1945.

But no such confession has ever come from the lips of the Roman Catholic hierarchy. When Pope John II visited Czechoslovakia in April 1990, he had a golden opportunity to visit Huss Square, where his spiritual predecessors burned John Huss at the stake simply because he refused to acknowledge the Roman Catholic blasphemy that priests are capable of creating our Lord's body and His blood in the Mass. The pope studiously avoided such a confession of wrong. This attitude stems from the papal dogma of infallibility, which protects the seeds of futher persecution when papal authority exercises the power that it had during the Middle Ages. Since she has never repented of the evil excesses that she has done in the past, she is capable of persecuting God's people again.

> They overcame him by the blood of the Lamb, and by the word of their testimony; and they loved not their lives unto the death (Revelation 12:11).

We must expect to see large numbers of professed Protestants capitulating to Roman Catholicism. This tragic trend is already accelerating; on the other hand, we must expect significant numbers of God's faithful people to leave the apostate churches, and join one fold under the bloodstained banner of Jesus Christ.

Before the return of Jesus, there comes a time when every human being's destiny is sealed. All have made an irrevocable decision for Jesus Christ or for Satan. A million years would not change that decision.

At that time, Christ will make His awesome pronouncement:

> He that is unjust, let him be unjust still: and he which is filthy, let him be filthy still: and he that is righteous, let him be righteous still: and he that is holy, let him be holy still (Revelation 22:11).

At this time, the Spirit of the Lord will no longer call people to repentance because there is no purpose in the Holy Spirit's appeal to the heart once each person's destiny is sealed. The Bible speaks about this time.

> There shall be a time of trouble, such as never was since there was a nation (Daniel 12:1).

The prophet, Jeremiah, also refers to this time.

> It is even the time of Jacob's trouble (Jeremiah 30:7).

At this time, the full fury of Satan will be turned upon God's faithful people in an attempt to eliminate them from the face of the earth. At that time, the effort to destroy God's people becomes universal. God pours out His judgments upon the earth during this period of vicious persecution. Many of these judgments, as recorded in Revelation 16, are directed against those who have worshiped the beast or are at the center of papal power. Two typical plagues are cited. There are seven in all.

> And the first went, and poured out his vial upon the earth; and there fell a noisome and grievous sore upon the men which had the mark of the beast, and upon them which worshipped his image (Revelation 16:2).

> And the fifth angel poured out his vial upon the seat of the beast; and his kingdom was full of darkness; and they gnawed their tongues for pain (Revelation 16:10).

Prior to the return of Jesus, Rome is destroyed.

> And the great city was divided into three parts, and the cities of the nations fell: and great Babylon came in remembrance before God, to give unto her the cup of the wine of the fierceness of his wrath (Revelation 16:19).

> And there followed another angel, saying, Babylon is fallen, is fallen, that great city, because she made all nations drink of the wine of the wrath of her fornication (Revelation 14:8).

At that time, God's saints who have been sustained only by His love and preserving power will see, with great rejoicing, the return of their long-awaited Lord and Redeemer.

> For the Lord himself shall descend from heaven with a shout, with the voice of the archangel, and with the trump of God: and the dead in Christ shall rise first: then we which are alive and remain shall be caught up together with them in the clouds, to meet the Lord in the air: and so shall we ever be with the Lord (1 Thessalonians 4:16, 17).

The promise of Jesus will be fulfilled:

> But he that shall endure unto the end, the same shall be saved (Matthew 24:13).

These saints have not worshiped the beast because they have fully surrendered their lives to Jesus, and their names are recorded in the Lamb's book of life (see Revelation 13:8).

The Lord is now calling all readers to total loyalty to Himself, so that their eternal destiny will be secure in the One who gave His life for the salvation of every human being.

21

A Moment to Decide

Before the creation of this earth, the eternal unity of the universe was split apart by the leader of the angels—Lucifer.

> How art thou fallen from heaven, O Lucifer, son of the morning! how art thou cut down to the ground, which didst weaken the nations! For thou hast said in thine heart, I will ascend into heaven, I will exalt my throne above the stars of God: I will sit also upon the mount of the congregation, in the sides of the north: I will ascend above the heights of the clouds; I will be like the most High (Isaiah 14:12-14).

In the form of a snake, Satan succeeded in destroying the loyalty of earth's first inhabitants to God.

> Now the serpent was more subtil than any beast of the field which the Lord God had made. And he said unto the woman, Yea, hath God said, Ye shall not eat of every tree of the garden? And the woman said unto the serpent, We may eat of the fruit of the trees of the garden: but of the fruit of the tree which is in the midst of the garden, God hath said, Ye shall not eat of it, neither shall ye touch it, lest ye die. And the serpent

said unto the woman, Ye shall not surely die: for God
doth know that in the day ye eat thereof, then your
eyes shall be opened, and ye shall be as gods, knowing good and evil. And when the woman saw that the
tree was good for food, and that it was pleasant to the
eyes, and a tree to be desired to make one wise, she
took of the fruit thereof, and did eat, and gave also
unto her husband with her; and he did eat (Genesis
3:1-6).

The issue, in the Garden of Eden, was a simple one—Eve
had the choice to accept the Word of God or the word of
the deceiver. Since then, that has been the issue. Today,
humanity faces the same decision—whether to accept the
Word of God, the One who is the truth {John 14:6} and
cannot lie {Titus 1:2}, or the word of Lucifer, Satan, the
father of lies {John 8:44}. The destiny of every human being
rests on this simple decision.

In one sense, Satan has always had an advantage over
God. God can only present truth, unadulterated and un-
modified. Satan can present an almost infinite combination
of truth and error. The battle is between the truth of God,
on the one hand, and the mixture of truth and error of
Satan, on the other. One willful step away from the truth of
God places us upon Satan's territory, and is sure to lead us
further into error of thought and action. There is only one
way to be totally committed to God.

Man doth not live by bread only, but by every word
that proceedeth out of the mouth of God
(Deuteronomy 8:3).

So many, today, have not understood that rejecting the
Word of God, even a small part of it, is dangerous to their
eternal salvation. While concentrating upon the mercy of

God, they have failed to give due acknowledgment to mercy's twin sister—justice. A just God could never trust a man or woman who has not been loyal to His Word to be a loyal citizen of heaven or of the new earth. The characteristics of the saints that will enter heaven are simply defined in Scripture.

> Here is the patience of the saints: here are they that keep the commandments of God, and the faith of Jesus (Revelation 14:12).

Placed in the setting of the time of the end, this text offers three unequivocal characteristics of those who accept the saving grace and mercy of Jesus. First, they have patience, or, as we would say today, endurance or perseverance. They do not yield their loyalty to God by compromising truth or Christian practice. They daily appropriate Christ's strength to obey everything that God says. These saints keep both the commandments of God and the faith of Jesus. While the antichrist has sought to change and depreciate the law of God, the saints cherish and obey it because they recognize that it is an exact transcript of the character of God. When we have the mind of Christ (Philippians 2:5), His character is revealed in us through the keeping of His commandments. But Paul reminds us that we cannot keep the commandments of God unless we also have the faith of Jesus.

> Whatsoever is not of faith is sin (Romans 14:23).

This faith enables us to believe that Jesus is completely able to save us, from sin, for His kingdom. Such a faith leads to victory over sin as our lives are constantly submitted to Jesus Christ. This faith is always demonstrated by obedience.

By faith Abel offered unto God a more excellent sacrifice than Cain, by which he obtained witness that he was righteous, God testifying of his gifts: and by it he being dead yet speaketh (Hebrews 11:4).

By faith Noah, being warned of God of things not seen as yet, moved with fear, prepared an ark to the saving of his house; by the which he condemned the world, and became heir of the righteousness which is by faith. By faith Abraham, when he was called to go out into a place which he should after receive for an inheritance, obeyed; and he went out, not knowing whither he went (Hebrews 11:7, 8).

By faith Moses, when he was come to years, refused to be called the son of Pharaoh's daughter; choosing rather to suffer affliction with the people of God, than to enjoy the pleasures of sin for a season (Hebrews 11:24, 25).

Throughout human history, millions have suffered persecution, deprivation, torture, imprisonment, and death rather than give up their loyalty to God. Such ultimate decisions are not hurriedly made, nor are they impulsive. God's faithful children have always been those who have developed the habit of daily submitting their wills and lives to Christ. They have allowed Jesus to guide them in every decision that they have made. As the Lord has permitted them to be tested on the little issues, they have leaned upon His strength for victory. The same strength is appropriated as more difficult tests come. Jesus has always been their strength and comfort because they fully believe the promises of God.

There hath no temptation taken you but such as is common to man: but God is faithful, who will not suffer you to be tempted above that ye are able; but will

with the temptation also make a way to escape, that
ye may be able to bear it (1 Corinthians 10:13).

Those who fail in the days of severe test and trial have
also failed earlier in the simple tests of life. They are often
oblivious to the fact that they are making decisions that are
of eternal consequence. They frequently wish to delay the
day of commitment, but such is usually a commitment that
is never made.

> How shall we escape, if we neglect so great salva-
> tion (Hebrews 2:3).

Knowing our tendency to indefinitely delay, He en-
courages us.

> To day if ye will hear his voice, harden not your
> hearts, as in the provocation (Hebrews 3:15).

Our minds immediately recall two tragic rulers who
sought to delay their response to the convicting power of
the Holy Spirit. As Paul, during his trial (following his arrest in Jerusalem), presented opportunities for salvation to
these leaders, their hearts stirred within them. Felix was
the first to witness Paul's powerful appeal.

> And as he [Paul] reasoned of righteousness,
> temperance, and judgment to come, Felix trembled,
> and answered, Go thy way for this time; when I have
> a convenient season, I will call for thee (Acts 24:25).

Tragically, there is no record that Felix ever made a
decision to follow Jesus during any *convenient season*. This
was Felix's only opportunity to decide.

Soon afterward, King Agrippa had his moment of
decision.

> King Agrippa, believest thou the prophets? I know
> that thou believest. Then Agrippa said unto Paul, Al-

most thou persuadest me to be a Christian (Acts 26:27, 28).

Again, there is no record that Agrippa was, at a later time, fully persuaded to be a Christian. His moment of eternal destiny was sealed at that moment. There is never an "almost." We either are under the banner of Christ or we are serving with the legions of the archrebel, Lucifer.

The importance of one decision can be seen in the lives of Daniel, Mishael, Azariah, and Hananiah. These four captives from Judah were destined for slavery; however, the most powerful potentate of the day, King Nebuchadnezzar, made the enlightened decision to train the elite of the captives for positions of rulership. The king even provided, for these young trainees, the same food and wine of which he partook. This decision of the four Jewish youths, not to violate their conscience, was to have profound implications throughout their lives. Daniel was obviously the leader in this decision.

> But Daniel purposed in his heart that he would not defile himself with the portion of the king's meat, nor with the wine which he drank: therefore he requested of the prince of the eunuchs that he might not defile himself (Daniel 1:8).

If these four men had not made this decision then, the book of Daniel would never have been written. The experiences, in chapters 3 and 6, would never have taken place as recorded. Hananiah (Shadrach), Mishael (Meshach), and Azariah (Abednego) would never have refused to bow to the golden image on the plain of Dura, with their lives at stake, if they had not earlier made their dietary decisions. Neither would Daniel have continued to audibly pray in front of his open window in defiance of the command, of King Darius, that all who worshiped another instead of the king would be thrown into the lions' den.

While God delivered His faithful servants in both these tests, deliverance may not always be God's plan. But whenever men and women have made the ultimate sacrifice, God has provided the strength to face even the cruelest of deaths. To the true Christian, loyalty to Christ has no conditions.

During the persecutions of the Middle Ages and the time of the Reformation, many nobly faced imprisonment and even martyrdom in their unswerving loyalty to proclaim the gospel of Jesus Christ. John Bunyan, famed author of *Pilgrim's Progress*, spent many years in prison because he refused to acknowledge the right of any human authority to authorize his preaching of the precious Word of God. A sympathetic judge did all he could to save Bunyan from prison. Aware of Bunyan's blind 2-year-old daughter, the judge offered to pardon him for preaching without ecclesiastical permission on condition that he agree not to do it again. But Bunyan said that he must preach by the authority of God. The judge then volunteered to arrange, with the Anglican Church, for him to receive approval to preach. Bunyan insisted that God had delegated this authority to no man except Jesus Himself. Sadly, the judge enforced the law of the day, and the faithful Bunyan was to survive many years in the dreary prison of Bedford.

Even more moving is the faithfulness of the sixteenth-century English martyr, Thomas Arthur. Arthur, too, was summoned for preaching without the permission of the

Roman Catholic Church. His words crystallized the courage that the proclaimers of the everlasting gospel will have at the end of time.

> Let our adversaries preach by the authority of the cardinal; others by the authority of the university; others by the popes; we will preach by the authority of God. It is not the man that brings the Word that saves the soul, but the Word which the man brings. Neither bishops nor popes have the right to forbid any man to preach the gospel; and if they kill him he is not a heretic, but a martyr (D'Aubigne, *The English Reformation*, vol. 1, p. 291).

Jesus foretold that God's faithful people will indeed face fearful persecution.

> If they have persecuted me, they will also persecute you; if they have kept my saying, they will keep yours also (John 15:20).

In many countries, this has already taken place. Whenever freedom of religion is violated, men and women have had to make quick decisions that have evidenced their loyalty or disloyalty to God. Frequently, the seventh-day Sabbath, of the fourth commandment in the decalogue, has been at stake. Only a small number have remained faithful to their Sabbathkeeping under threats of confiscation, separation from family, imprisonment, torture, death, and when civil authorities have demanded that they send their children to school on Sabbath or work on God's holy, sacred day.

In 1972, a woman in East Germany faced the ultimate decision—send her 8-year-old daughter (her only child) to school on Sabbath or have her removed by civil authorities. In spite of her prayers, the child was taken away. But God had not forgotten her. When a plaque that declared her to be an unfit mother was posted in the center of the woman's village, the villagers rallied to her plight. They proclaimed her to be one of the finest mothers in the village; also, they forced the officials to return the girl to her mother by refusing to do any work assignment for the government until this was done. The child was returned to her mother. What a great God we serve!

In another country that was swept by revolution, a Christian press was taken over by the revolutionaries. Immediately, the Sabbathkeeping staff was required to work on Sabbath, at the risk of execution if they refused to obey. All workers capitulated except one pressman who placed his loyalty to God above his own life. When he reported to work on Monday, he was given one more chance to show his loyalty to the revolution by working the next Sabbath. He refused, and immediately the execution squad was summoned to take him to the place of execution. As he was being roughly taken out of the door of the press building, the revolutionary chief abruptly called him back and informed him he had his Sabbaths free from work. When the other workers heard about what had happened, they entreated the chief for the same consideration, but were greeted only by the angry response, "Get out of here!" They had lost their moment to decide for Christ.

In recent times, we have seen efforts to establish Sunday laws. It has been a characteristic of communist countries to require work and school attendance every day of the week, excluding Sunday. This has created untold hardships for faithful Sabbathkeepers. As a result, many were imprisoned. Some had their children taken from them. And some died as martyrs to their faith. Two islands in the free world (Fiji and Puerto Rico) led the way, in the late 1980s, in legislating Sunday laws that prevented normal activities on Sunday. It has been well-known that Sabbath observance will become the final test of loyalty to God just prior to the second coming of Jesus.

During September 1989 in the United States, a chilling warning was given to Sabbathkeeping Christians when the First Circuit Court of Appeals, in Boston, upheld the validity of the Puerto Rican Sunday closing laws. Once again, the court system of the United States demonstrated its readiness to enforce legislation that is designed to place special significance upon the pagan day of the sun. This court opinion certainly renewed the intention of activist groups, such as the Lord's Day Alliance, to apply pressure for Sunday closing laws to be enacted by legislatures on the mainland of the Unites States. It is more likely that such laws will be enacted in a time of great national need or crisis.

People of other races have a much tougher mentality than those in the Western cultures. It will require a total commitment to Christ in order for faithful people to stand the tests and trials that are just ahead of us. Only those who daily study God's Word, and, under the power of the Holy Spirit, apply these truths to their lives will prove faithful. Now is the time to make your decision for Christ. Even though the test of loyalty will encompass every facet of our lives, the Sabbath test will rivet the attention of the world to the challenge of God's authority and rulership. As we approach the time when the image to the beast is fully formed, now is a time to make decisions for truth and righteousness. As the fury of the antichrist reaches its apex, only those who are secure in the power of Jesus Christ will stand faithful. The decision made then will depend upon the decisions made now. There can be no neutrality then, anymore than God allows neutrality now.

> He that is not with me is against me; and he that gathereth not with me scattereth abroad (Matthew 12:30).

We realize that this book will bring, to many readers, the challenge of their lifetime. We believe no one can read it without being brought, like Felix and Agrippa, to a decision in his or her life. We pray that your decision, renewed every day, will be to join the faithful group of God's loyal remnant. The King's return is close at hand. Be ready "to meet the Lord in the air" (1 Thessalonians 4:17). Be ready to join the triumphant band in their shout of victory.

> And it shall be said in that day, Lo, this is our God; we have waited for him, and he will save us: this is the Lord; we have waited for him, we will be glad and rejoice in his salvation (Isaiah 25:9).

This page intentionally left blank.

22

Come Out of Her, My People

The final divine call to humanity provides the urgent invitation to separate from the Roman Catholic Church and the fallen Protestant churches which have adopted her apostasy.

> And I heard another voice from heaven, saying, Come out of her, my people, that ye be not partakers of her sins, and that ye receive not of her plagues. For her sins have reached unto heaven, and God hath remembered her iniquities (Revelation 18:4, 5).

This call comes with the everlasting gospel that is proclaimed to all the inhabitants of the earth. Jesus gave His disciples a precious promise when they asked Him when the end of the world would be.

> And this gospel of the kingdom shall be preached in all the world for a witness unto all nations; and then shall the end come (Matthew 24:14).

That promise has always been the dynamic force that has motivated Christ's true followers to proclaim His message of love, salvation, and soon coming to this world. Jesus was not dealing in general terms because He said "*this* gospel," not "*a* gospel." Evidently, this was not a temporary or transitory gospel. This gospel is most clearly defined, in Revelation 14, in what is frequently referred to as the first angel's message, which is part of the other two messages that follow.

> And I saw another angel fly in the midst of heaven, having the everlasting gospel to preach unto them that dwell on the earth, and to every nation, and kindred, and tongue, and people, saying with a loud voice, Fear God, and give glory to him; for the hour of his judgment is come: and worship him that made heaven, and earth, and the sea, and the fountains of waters (Revelation 14:6, 7).

It is one thing to be called out of Babylon; it is another thing to know where to go. When the Jews were given the opportunity to leave literal Babylon, many remained. So it will be when the final invitation is given. God will have an authentic church with His true believers. The book of Revelation frequently refers to the pure woman at the endtime. Such symbolism is always representative of God's true, pure church.

> And there appeared a great wonder in heaven; *a woman clothed with the sun*, and the moon under her feet, and upon her head a crown of twelve stars (Revelation 12:1, emphasis added).

> And the dragon was wroth with *the woman*, and went to make war with the remnant of her seed, which keep the commandments of God, and have the testimony of Jesus Christ (Revelation 12:17, emphasis added).

> And the Spirit and *the bride* say, Come. And let him that heareth say, Come. And let him that is athirst come. And whosoever will, let him take the water of life freely (Revelation 22:17, emphasis added).

It is self-evident that it will be this church which will give the invitation of Revelation 18:4 to the world. It will present the everlasting gospel of Revelation 14:6, 7 to earth's inhabitants. Those honest souls who reach the conviction that they are members of a church from which God is calling them now have the opportunity to join that group of people who will take this everlasting gospel to the world.

It is essential that we discover the message of the everlasting gospel, and discern which church espouses it in its fullness. The everlasting gospel is to be known, believed, lived, and proclaimed. A review of Revelation 14:7 reveals that there are four interwoven elements of this message:

1. Fear God.

2. Give glory to Him.

3. The hour of His judgment is come.

4. Worship Him that made heaven, and earth, and the sea, and the fountains of waters.

An understanding of these principles will reveal the church that has accepted these truths. It is possible that some readers will not possess a thorough understanding of the meaning of each of these components. We will use the good Protestant principle of biblical interpretation as we explore the Scriptures because the Bible surely is its own best expositor, the only flawless guide to its own meaning.

1. *Fear God.* John, the author of Revelation, undoubtedly was a great student of the Old Testament because he frequently quoted from it. The book of Revelation, in many places, parallels the book of Daniel and other Old Testament prophecies. John acquired his concept of godly fear from what he read in the Old Testament. Consequently, we must turn to the Old Testament in order to discover the broad scope of the command to fear God.

The experience of Abraham, when he was about to offer Isaac on Mount Moriah, clarifies the meaning of implicit and unwavering obedience to God's command.

> And he said, Lay not thine hand upon the lad, neither do thou any thing unto him: for now I know that thou *fearest God*, seeing thou hast not withheld thy son, thine only son from me (Genesis 22:12, emphasis added).

These words are of major significance because they were spoken by Christ Himself. Since the book of Revelation is the revelation of Jesus Christ (Revelation 1:1), consistency requires that we apply the same meaning to the use of the same term in each passage.

Abraham's faith was so firm that he obeyed God's awesome request, and believed that God could and would raise his boy from the dead. He believed this despite the fact that there is no inspired record that a single human had ever been raised from the dead prior to the Mount Moriah experience. This, in reality, was absolute faith that was manifested by unquestioning obedience to our God.

> By faith Abraham, when he was tried, offered up Isaac: and he that had received the promises offered up his only begotten son, of whom it was said, That in

Isaac shall thy seed be called: accounting that God was able to raise him up, even from the dead; from whence also he received him in a figure (Hebrews 11:17-19).

In the book of Deuteronomy, Moses explained the meaning of the requirement to fear God.

That thou mightest fear the Lord thy God, to keep all his statutes and his commandments, which I command thee (Deuteronomy 6:2).

Therefore thou shalt keep the commandments of the Lord thy God, to walk in his ways, and to fear him (Deuteronomy 8:6).

And now, Israel, what doth the Lord thy God require of thee, but to fear the Lord thy God, to walk in all his ways, and to love him, and to serve the Lord thy God with all thy heart and with all thy soul, to keep the commandments of the Lord, and his statutes, which I command thee this day for thy good (Deuteronomy 10:12, 13)?

These passages call God's people to obey the law of God and His Word. To fear God is to so implicitly trust God that our lives will not reflect our own fallible, human judgment. Instead, we will be ready to follow God's leading whatever it may be. Only such a people will be able to be used by God to take the everlasting gospel to every nook and cranny of this world.

They overcame him [Satan] by the blood of the lamb, and by the word of their testimony; and they loved not their lives unto the death (Revelation 12:11).

The Roman Catholic Church is not the only church that refuses to acknowledge God's power to keep His people from falling into sin. Most Protestant churches today deny that God's people will possess perfection of character before Christ returns. The Bible is replete with assurances that, in His power, Christ's humble flock will overcome all sin. In confirmation of this fact, we cite a selection of passages from Holy Writ.

> For what the law could not do, in that it was weak through the flesh, God sending his own Son in the likeness of sinful flesh, and for sin, condemned sin in the flesh: that the righteousness of the law might be fulfilled in us, who walk not after the flesh, but after the Spirit (Romans 8:3, 4).

> If we confess our sins, he is faithful and just to forgive us our sins, and to cleanse us from all unrighteousness (1 John 1:9).

> For the grace of God that bringeth salvation hath appeared to all men, teaching us that, denying ungodliness and worldly lusts, we should live soberly, righteously, and godly, in this present world (Titus 2:11, 12).

> Wherefore he is able also to save them to the uttermost that come unto God by him, seeing he ever liveth to make intercession for them (Hebrews 7:25).

> Forasmuch then as Christ hath suffered for us in the flesh, arm yourselves likewise with the same mind: for he that hath suffered in the flesh hath ceased from sin; that he no longer should live the rest of his time in the flesh to the lusts of men, but to the will of God (1 Peter 4:1, 2).

Many have a form of godliness but do not possess the genuine love for God that is so essential for those who are seeking to serve Him.

> Having a form of godliness, but denying the power thereof: from such turn away (2 Timothy 3:5).

Such will not receive the crown of life. It must be remembered that we cannot, by our human effort, have day-by-day victory over sin. It is the grace of God that provides such strength.

> For the grace of God that bringeth salvation hath appeared to all men (Titus 2:11).

Only Christ, the victorious One, can keep us from falling.

> Now unto him that is able to keep you from falling, and to present you faultless before the presence of his glory with exceeding joy (Jude 24).

He has promised that those who have submitted their will to Him will not be tested above their endurance.

> There hath no temptation taken you but such as is common to man: but God is faithful, who will not suffer you to be tempted above that ye are able; but will with the temptation also make a way to escape, that ye may be able to bear it (1 Corinthians 10:13).

A daily commitment of our lives to Jesus requires us to truly fear God. Freedom from the enslavement of sin is the greatest blessing that God desires to give us.

2. *Give glory to Him.* At first thought, it would seem impossible that fallen humans could give any glory to the God of the universe. God possesses infinite glory, and we innately possess none. Glory represents character. Adam and Eve lost their garments of light when their characters were marred by sin. The all-perfect One surely possesses infinite glory. We must trust the Lord that somehow we will be empowered to "give glory to Him." The Bible does not leave us in ignorance. Jesus Himself addressed the issue.

> Let your light so shine before men, that they may
> see your good works, and glorify your Father which is
> in heaven (Matthew 5:16).

Righteous characters reflect works of righteousness. Our works must always be for the glory of God, and never for ourselves. Paul's writings add another dimension to this command to "give glory to Him."

> Whether therefore ye eat, or drink, or whatsoever
> ye do, do all to the glory of God (1 Corinthians 10:31).

Even in our daily food and drink, our dietary habits, we need to reflect the glory of God. Paul also tells us that we are the temple of God.

> Know ye not that ye are the temple of God, that the
> Spirit of God dwelleth in you? If any man defile the
> temple of God, him shall God destroy; for the temple
> of God is holy, which temple ye are (1 Corinthians
> 3:16, 17).

> What? know ye not that your body is the temple of
> the Holy Ghost which is in you, which ye have of
> God, and ye are not your own? For ye are bought with
> a price: therefore glorify God in your body, and in
> your spirit, which are God's (1 Corinthians 6:19, 20).

> And what agreement hath the temple of God with
> idols? for ye are the temple of the living God; as God
> hath said, I will dwell in them, and walk in them; and
> I will be their God, and they shall be my people.
> Wherefore come out from among them, and be ye
> separate, saith the Lord, and touch not the unclean
> thing: and I will receive you (2 Corinthians 6:16, 17).

Note the striking relationship between 2 Corinthians 6:16, 17 and idolatry. The image worship of the Roman Catholic Church can never lead to God dwelling in the human temple.

Referring back to 1 Corinthians 10:31, it is evident that our health habits need to reflect the glory of God. Many churches have given little heed to the relationship of biblical health habits to Christian character; also, they have not taken a stand against alcohol or tobacco. They do not educate their members in those dietary principles which will enhance their Christian commitment, service, and honor to God. It is evident that God's faithful church will practice these true health principles.

God's true end-time church will teach the commandments of God and claim Christ's provision to keep His faithful servants from falling back into sin. They will also honor God with their habits of a healthy lifestyle. Sadly, most churches of Protestantism do not measure up to these requirements.

3. *The hour of His judgment is come.* This judgment hour message is little understood in Christendom. It cannot be understood by most Christians because they have accepted the Greek-pagan concept of immediate life after death that has been consistently taught since the time of the ancient city of Babylon. The Bible consistently teaches that death is a dreamless sleep. Each deceased person awaits the call of the Life-giver at His second coming.

> For the living know that they shall die: but the dead know not any thing, neither have they any more a reward; for the memory of them is forgotten (Ecclesiastes 9:5).

> Whatsoever thy hand findeth to do, do it with thy might; for there is no work, nor device, nor knowledge, nor wisdom, in the grave, whither thou goest (Ecclesiastes 9:10).

And many of them that sleep in the dust of the earth shall awake, some to everlasting life, and some to shame and everlasting contempt (Daniel 12:2).

These things said he: and after that he said unto them, Our friend Lazarus sleepeth; but I go, that I may awake him out of sleep. Then said his disciples, Lord, if he sleep, he shall do well. Howbeit Jesus spake of his death: but they thought that he had spoken of taking of rest in sleep (John 11:11-13).

Behold, I shew you a mystery; We shall not all sleep, but we shall all be changed   (1 Corinthians 15:51).

For if we believe that Jesus died and rose again, even so them also which sleep in Jesus will God bring with him (1 Thessalonians 4:14).

Job recognized that he would see God in his flesh instead of in a spirit body.

And though after my skin worms destroy this body, yet in my flesh shall I see God (Job 19:26).

God's reference to *souls* means living humans who sin and will be destroyed if they do not repent of their sins. There is no indication of eternal punishment in Scripture.

Behold, all souls are mine; as the soul of the father, so also the soul of the son is mine: the soul that sinneth, it shall die (Ezekiel 18:4).

The Bible plainly states that only God possesses immortality.

Who only hath immortality, dwelling in the light which no man can approach unto; whom no man hath seen, nor can see: to whom be honour and power everlasting (1 Timothy 6:16).

The Word of God teaches that the faithful receive immortality only at the resurrection of the righteous dead.

> Behold, I shew you a mystery; We shall not all sleep, but we shall all be changed, in a moment, in the twinkling of an eye, at the last trump: for the trumpet shall sound, and the dead shall be raised incorruptible, and we shall be changed. For this corruptible must put on incorruption, and this mortal must put on immortality (1 Corinthians 15:51-53).

The Bible teaches that man is presently mortal.

Jesus wished to give His disciples the hope of eternal life. He did not point them to the moment of their deaths; instead, He directed their minds to His second coming—the time when they would be resurrected. Study this passage carefully.

> Let not your heart be troubled: ye believe in God, believe also in me. In my Father's house are many mansions: if it were not so, I would have told you. I go to prepare a place for you. And if I go and prepare a place for you, I will come again, and receive you unto myself; that where I am, there ye may be also (John 14:1-3).

God, in His infinite wisdom, allows His fallen creation to rest in the grave until He calls them forth in the resurrection; thus God's redeemed are spared the agony of observing the effects of sin upon their living loved ones. In His justice, God allows the unfallen angels of the universe to review the records of the human race before one soul is saved.

> I beheld till the thrones were cast down, and the Ancient of days did sit, whose garment was white as snow, and the hair of his head like the pure wool: his

> throne was like the fiery flame, and his wheels as
> burning fire. A fiery stream issued and came forth
> from before him: thousand thousands ministered unto
> him, and ten thousand times ten thousand stood
> before him: the judgment was set, and the books were
> opened (Daniel 7:9, 10).

John identifies these myriads of beings as multitudes of
angels who are present at the judgment.

> And I beheld, and I heard the voice of many angels
> round about the throne and the beasts and the elders:
> and the number of them was ten thousand times ten
> thousand, and thousands of thousands (Revelation
> 5:11).

This judgment is presently in progress in heaven. It takes
place just prior to the return of Jesus. Daniel refers to the
establishment of Christ's kingdom that is immediately after
the judgment of the beast power.

> And there was given him [Christ] dominion, and
> glory, and a kingdom, that all people, nations, and
> languages, should serve him: his dominion is an ever-
> lasting dominion, which shall not pass away, and his
> kingdom that which shall not be destroyed (Daniel
> 7:14).

In this judgment, all who have claimed loyalty to God
are judged. God formally declares who are His faithful
people. It is important to note that this judgment begins
just after the end of the medieval reign of the papacy.
Daniel mentions the papal power.

> And he shall speak great words against the most
> High, and shall wear out the saints of the most High,
> and think to change times and laws: and they shall be
> given into his hand until a time and times and the
> dividing of time. But the judgment shall sit, and they

shall take away his dominion, to consume and to destroy it unto the end (Daniel 7:25, 26).

The 1260 days were indeed symbolic of the 1260 years of papal dominance over Europe. (See chapter 5, entitled "The Medieval Reign of the Papacy.") This time period began in 538 when Pope Vigilius exercised the role of Pontifex Maximus, and concluded with Pope Pius VI's imprisonment in 1798. This prophecy, the 1260-year period of papal domiance is represented by the term, *a time, and times, and half a time*, literally one year, two years, and half a year, or 1260 prophetic days (1260 literal years).

The papacy (here represented by the little horn) will be judged as unfaithful, and all those who worship him will similarly be judged as unfaithful. This same judgment considers the lives of God's people.

> And at that time shall Michael stand up, the great prince which standeth for the children of thy people: and there shall be a time of trouble, such as never was since there was a nation even to that same time: and at that time thy people shall be delivered, every one that shall be found written in the book (Daniel 12:1).

> Until the Ancient of days came, and judgment was given to [in favor of] the saints of the most High; and the time came that the saints possessed the kingdom (Daniel 7:22).

God's judgment is against the little horn (the papacy) and in favor of His people. What a wonderful message this is to the world. Christ stands up for His people in the judgment. It would be a fearful experience to have to stand alone before God's judgment bar without the One who lived a perfect life and died for our salvation. Our Lord, our Saviour, stands up for us in the judgment. What a thrilling prospect! Both authors have preached this message around the world, and both have thrilled at the response of Protestants, Catholics, Christians, and non-Christians to this message.

We have found only one church that preaches this message—the Seventh-day Adventist Church. We have been especially blessed to recognize that this church also upholds the Bible principle that declares that God's saints will keep the commandments of God through the faith of Jesus.

> Here is the patience of the saints: here are they that keep the commandments of God, and the faith of Jesus (Revelation 14:12).

We also realize that this church has, for well-over a century, placed emphasis upon the message of healthful living.

4. *Worship Him that made heaven, and earth, and the sea, and the fountains of waters.* This final facet of the everlasting gospel calls for worship of the Creator. This command incorporates an explicit reference to the Sabbath commandment.

> Remember the sabbath day, to keep it holy. Six days shalt thou labour, and do all thy work: but the seventh day is the sabbath of the Lord thy God: in it thou shalt not do any work, thou, nor thy son, nor thy daughter, thy manservant, nor thy maidservant, nor thy cattle, nor thy stranger that is within thy gates: for in six days the Lord made heaven and earth, the sea, and all that in them is, and rested the seventh day: wherefore the Lord blessed the sabbath day, and hallowed it (Exodus 20:8-11).

There is only one day that God has ordained as the reminder of His creative power—the seventh day of the week.

> And on the seventh day God ended his work which he had made; and he rested on the seventh day from all his work which he had made. And God blessed the seventh day, and sanctified it: because that in it he had rested from all his work which God created and made (Genesis 2:2, 3).

This day was honored by the ancient patriarchs and re-established by Moses. God is particular. It is not within man's province to determine the day which should be hallowed.

> And it came to pass, that on the sixth day they gathered twice as much bread, two omers for one man: and all the rulers of the congregation came and told Moses. And he said unto them, This is that which the Lord hath said, To morrow is the rest of the holy sabbath unto the Lord: bake that which ye will bake to day, and seethe that ye will seethe; and that which remaineth over lay up for you to be kept until the morning (Exodus 16:22, 23).

This day was set aside as a sign or seal (see Romans 4:11) of sanctification.

> Speak thou also unto the children of Israel, saying, Verily my sabbaths ye shall keep: for it is a sign between me and you throughout your generations; that ye may know that I am the Lord that doth sanctify you (Exodus 31:13).

> Moreover also I gave them my sabbaths, to be a sign between me and them, that they might know that I am the Lord that sanctify them (Ezekiel 20:12).

This day was kept by the faithful throughout the Old Testament era. Christ worshiped on this day when He was on earth.

> And he came to Nazareth, where he had been brought up: and, as his custom was, he went into the synagogue on the sabbath day, and stood up for to read (Luke 4:16).

Christ claimed this day as His very own.

> Therefore the Son of man is Lord also of the sabbath (Mark 2:28).

Paul also worshiped on this day.

> And he reasoned in the synagogue every sabbath, and persuaded the Jews and the Greeks (Acts 18:4).

During life in the new earth, all of God's redeemed will worship Him on that special day.

> And it shall come to pass, that from one new moon to another, and from one sabbath to another, shall all flesh come to worship before me, saith the Lord (Isaiah 66:23).

Some Christians who are not very knowledgeable about the Scriptures have questioned whether Saturday is the Sabbath that is referred to in the fourth commandment. The Bible establishes this fact in relation to the death and resurrection of Jesus Christ. Jesus died on what has become known as Good Friday, and rose from the dead on Easter Sunday. There is only one day between these two days—Saturday. Luke refers to the day of Christ's death (Friday).

> And that day was the preparation, and the Sabbath drew on (Luke 23:54).

The Sabbath was observed, in Christ's day, from sunset on Friday evening and extended to sunset on Saturday evening, as God had commanded; thus, when Jesus died at 3 p.m. on Friday, it was still the preparation day, and the Sabbath soon followed.

Matthew recorded the day of Christ's resurrection (Sunday).

> In the end of the Sabbath, as it began to dawn toward the first day of the week, came Mary Magdalene and the other Mary to see the sepulchre. And, behold, there was a great earthquake: for the angel of the Lord descended from heaven, and came and rolled back the stone from the door, and sat upon it (Matthew 28:1, 2).

Scripture decisively declares that the Sabbath is indeed Saturday. History testifies to the fact that no alteration in the weekly cycle has occurred since apostolic times.

This was the day upon which most of the faithful Christians, up to at least the seventh century (see chapter 5, entitled "The Medieval Reign of the Papacy"), worshiped. We recognize that the Roman Catholic Church proudly boasts that it was not Christ or the apostles who changed the Sabbath from the seventh day (Saturday) to the first day (Sunday). As previously mentioned, many gave their lives in loyalty to their Creator. At the end of time, the Sabbath will once more become the great test of loyalty to Christ.

Satan hates the Sabbath because it is an acknowledgment of the One to whom we justifiably owe total allegiance. Ever since the controversy in heaven, Satan has sought to claim the rulership of this world. Worship on the pagan day of the sun is an acknowledgment of Satan's rulership. One shows, by what day he worships, his loyalty to the sovereignty of the Creator in their lives. God desires to recreate His image in our hearts.

As its name attests, the Seventh-day Adventist Church teaches the eternal, unchangeable law of God and Jesus' provisions for keeping it; the healthful lifestyle of the Bible; and the judgment-hour message. It also teaches men and women to acknowledge their loyalty to Christ by keeping holy His sacred seventh day.

The authors were born into an undivided Seventh-day Adventist family; however, in their youth, they challenged every truth that the Seventh-day Adventist Church taught. By earnest prayerful study of God's Word, we were compelled to acknowledge that the Seventh-day Adventist Church, and that church alone, proclaims the truth of the everlasting gospel. It alone can be trusted to take the gospel to the world, under the power of the Holy Spirit. We encourage all faithful Christians—Catholics and Protestants alike—to unite with God's remnant church, the Seventh-day Adventist Church. The same sincere invitation is extended to all non-Christians.

The reader might well ask, "Is the Seventh-day Adventist Church a perfect church?" The answer to this question is an emphatic "No." It is under fearful assault today because of its loyalty to Christ and His gospel. Many of its members and even ministers have wavered from the everlasting gospel. Other church members are indifferent. Still others have become enemies of the gospel while they seek to retain their membership in the Seventh-day Adventist

Church. Both the authors are ordained ministers of the Seventh-day Adventist Church, and well-know that large numbers of nominal adherents have failed to present God's gospel truth. If such apostasy and indifference were not found in God's church just prior to our Lord's return, Scripture would not be accurate. But, irrespective of this fact, the Seventh-day Adventist Church is the only depository of God's truth on earth today. The Bible details a fearful sifting and shaking of God's people at the end of time. We are presently in that time.

> For, lo, I will command, and I will sift the house of Israel among all nations, like as corn is sifted in a sieve, yet shall not the least grain fall upon the earth (Amos 9:9).

> And I will shake all nations, and the desire of all nations shall come: and I will fill this house with glory, saith the Lord of hosts (Haggai 2:7).

Many will worship the beast and his image, but God will bring His sheep, from all faiths, into His fold. The wheat and tares grow together until the end-time. While many who are presently within the Seventh-day Adventist Church will fail and leave the church during the final test, it can be expected that multitudes of faithful men and women will join its fellowship. We invite you, the reader, to be one of these.

We will also be glad to hear from you. We pray that God will abundantly bless you as you seek to follow in the humble footsteps of your Lord and Saviour. This is not a frivolous decision. Those who are seeking to follow Christ have only one alternative—to honor His Lordship by worshiping on His sacred Sabbath day. The invitation is *now* extended to all who are seeking to join that church which will unitedly take the everlasting gospel, as presented in Revelation 14:6-12, to every nation, kindred, tongue, and people.

For further information concerning the gospel that is being taught by the Seventh-day Adventist Church, it may be obtained through free Bible study guides by writing to Hartland Institute, Box 1, Rapidan, Virginia 22733, U.S.A.

It is the earnest prayer of both authors that each reader will accept the great salvation of our Saviour.

Other Interesting Books and Videos

Books

Family Crisis in America $5.95
> The biblical principles of mental health.

The Sacrificial Priest **$5.95**
> The biblical foundation of the sanctuary message.

Youth, Do You Dare! **$4.95**
> Gives insights to help them strengthen the values and spiritual dimentions of their lives.

Second Coming, Fervent Hope or Faded Dream . . . **$4.95**

Inspirational VHS Videos (approximately four hours each video)

"Education for Today." Three videos at **$54.95**. Discussion on discipline, entertainment, parenting, competition, and other topics by Dr. Standish.

Roundtable on Health with Peters, Goley, Wilson (2 tape set) **$49.00** (single) **$25.00**

Lifestyle to Health Series with Drs. Peters, Wilson, Goley (4 tape set) **$95.00**.

On cancer, and other topics **$18.88**
On sugar, disease, and other topics **$18.88**
On exercise, anger, and other topics **$18.88**
On hydrotherapy, and other topics **$18.88**

Vegetarian Cookbooks

Hartland Heartsavers **$4.95**
Eat for Strength, Regular by A. Thrash **$7.95**
Eat for Strength, Oil Free by A. Thrash **$7.95**
The Joy of Cooking Naturally by P. Dameron **$9.95**
Cooking With Natural Foods by M. Beltz **$14.95**
Weimar Cookbook **$7.95**
Of These Ye May Freely Eat by J. Rachor **$2.95**
Strict Vegetarian Cookbook by L. Tadej **$7.95**
Something Better by E. Earl & N. Brackett **$8.95**

Like to Tell You More About . . .

College

An opportunity to learn in a country setting with Christ-centered classes, work education, and outreach ministries. Majors: Pastoral Evangelism, Christian Elementary and Secondary Education, Christian Business Administration, Bible Worker Training, Restaurant Management, and Health Ministries. Contact dean of school. **Phone** 703-672-3100.

Lifestyle Reconditioning Center

A friendly and relaxing atmosphere, with qualified health-care professionals who are skilled in promotimg lifestyle intervention for those who suffer from heart disease, arthritus, cancer, diabeties, overweight, and other conditions.

Bible Conferences

Meetings scheduled, in various locations, concerning the topics of evangelism, doctrines, and health seminars. Contact Hartland Bible Conference coordinator. **Phone** 703-672-3100.

Hartland Journal

Information about what God is doing for us, as well as articles on physical and spiritual health.

Institute Publications

Books, inspirational cassetes, and videos for serious Christians. Catalog with price list available. Visa and MasterCard accepted. **Phone** 703-672-3566.

Volunteer Opportunities

Short and long term opportunities available for those who would like to volunteer their time and talents in exchange for food, lodging, and blessings from fellowship with volunteers, health guests, students, and staff. Contact business manager. **Phone** 703-672-3100.

Weekend Retreats and Campmeetings at Hartland

Schedule available upon request. Contact retreat and campmeeting coordinator. **Phone** 703-672-3100.

Last Generation
The Silent Messenger!

What is *Last Generation* magazine?

- A bimonthly publication dedicated to preparing this generation to meet Jesus at His soon return.
- A witnessing resource written especially for individuals asking spiritual questions.

What subjects does *Last Generation* feature?

- News events in the light of prophecy.
- Topical Bible study with last day emphasis.
- Health and fitness.
- The Christian walk.
- Contemporary issues such as music, drugs, entertainment, dating, and marraige.

What format does *Last Generation* use?

- 32 glossy pages with many color illustrations.
- Short, fast moving articles.

How can I use *Last Generation* for witnessing?

- Sponsor gift subscriptions to friends, family members, work associates, prisons, waiting rooms, libraries, and schools.
- Place in liturature racks and public areas.
- Use in door-to-door evangelism.
- Sponsor magazines to English speaking peoples in Africa and the Far East.

How can I send/or recieve *Last Generation*?

- Fill out the order blank below and mail to our office.
- Or call 1-800-763-9355 for more information. Have your VISA or MasterCard handy.

Costs only US$9.95 for 6 issues. Canada:US$9.95. Overseas surface: US$14.95.

Gift subs to more than one address: Please pay in US $: 2@8.95 ea.; 3@7.95 ea.; 4@6.95 ea.; 5-9@6.50 ea.; 10-24@6.00 ea.; 25-49@5.75 ea.; 50-99@5.50 ea.; 100 or more@5.00 ea. Please add US$ 5.00 to cover postage for each overseas subscription.

Bulk single issue to one address: .65/magazine plus postage to your address. Case price of single or mixed issues is US$100 plus shipping to your address.

I would like to recieve and/or send subscriptions to the following addresses:

Name_____   Name_____
Address_____   Address_____
City_____State_____   City_____State_____
Zip_____Country____   Zip_____Country____

Please send additional names and addresses on a separate sheet of paper.
Payment enclosed (check or money order) or amount ordered:_____
VISA or MasterCard #_____Exp. date_____

Call or write for your complementary copy!